ARIZONA

THE GRAND CANYON STATE

BY STEVEN L. WALKER

Above: Saguaro cactus in bloom. The flower of the Saguaro is Arizona's State Flower.
PHOTO BY JERRY JACKA

Front, back and inside front covers:
Owl-clover, *Orthocarpus purpurascens,* in bloom at Organ Pipe National Monument.
PHOTO BY BOB CLEMENZ

A view of Mount Hayden from Point Imperial on the North Rim of the Grand Canyon.
PHOTO BY DICK DIETRICH

Sedona's Cathedral Rock towers above Oak Creek at Red Rock Crossing.
PHOTO BY BOB CLEMENZ

The Arizona state flag design on a hot-air balloon above the Granite Dells. PHOTO BY G. JOHNSON

CAMELBACK DESIGN GROUP, INC.   **CANYONLANDS** PUBLICATIONS & INDIAN ART

Designed by Camelback Design Group, Inc., 8655 East Via de Ventura, Suite G200, Scottsdale, Arizona 85258. Phone: 602-948-4233. Distributed by Canyonlands Publications, 4860 North Ken Morey Drive, Bellemont, Arizona 86015. For ordering information please call (520) 779-3888.

Printed in South Korea
Library of Congress Catalog Number: 91-71505
International Standard Book Number: 1-879924-00-5

Published in the United States of America.

GEOGRAPHY

Arizona, with a total area approaching 114,000 square miles, is the sixth largest state. Bordered by New Mexico on the east, California and Nevada to the west, Utah at the top and Mexico along the southern border, Arizona is 392 miles at its widest point from north to south and 338 miles from east to west. The Four Corners area in the northeast corner of the state is the only place in the country where borders of four neighboring states meet at one point.

Within the state there is a wide variety of landscapes, climates, flora and fauna. Elevation ranges from a low point near Yuma, at 70 feet above sea level, to Mount Humphreys, one of the San Francisco Peaks, at 12,670 feet. Rainfall varies from around three inches annually in parts of the desert region to more than 30 inches a year in the highest mountains.

Temperatures range from extreme heat in the desert during summer, with June 15, 1896 and July 7, 1905 both posting 127°F, to bone chilling cold spells, with Hawley Lake reaching -40°F on January 7, 1971.

These wide variations in temperature, rain and elevation have created three distinct physiographic zones: the northern plateau, the mountain region and the desert. The northern plateau is a high-elevation northeastern plain containing many of the state's most unusual geological formations, including the Grand Canyon, Petrified Forest and Painted Desert. The mountain region is a central mountain belt crossing diagonally from the northwest to the southeast. The desert region is in the southwestern area of the state.

The northern plateau is part of the Colorado Plateau and is divided into sections by the canyons of the Colorado and Little Colorado rivers. The Arizona Strip, a section north of the Grand Canyon, includes the Kaibab Forest and is sparsely developed. The plateau section to the south of the Grand Canyon contains the San Francisco Peaks, Meteor Crater and the largest contiguous stand of Ponderosa Pine in the world. The Navajo section of the northern plateau is an arid area containing the Navajo Reservation, Hopi villages, Painted Desert, Petrified Forest and Monument Valley.

The mountain region extends into Mexico where it becomes the Sierra Madres. Although each region contains some mountains, the mountain region is home to the major mountain attractions. Cooler summer temperatures draws throngs of desert dwellers in summer months and winter snowfall attracts legions of skiers during the winter.

The desert region is the most populous and is responsible for a majority of the commerce conducted in the state. Irrigation has made large farming operations possible. The greater Phoenix and Tucson metropolitan areas are major tourist attractions to winter visitors. The desert region also houses the state capital, Phoenix, two of the state's major universities, and its professional sports teams.

Located in the southwestern United States, Arizona's contrasts in scenery, climates and cultures make it one of the nation's most popular destinations. From the mountain highlands to the low desert valleys, Arizona contains each of the seven life zones found in North America; a wide variety of flora and fauna; geological formations that are found nowhere else in the world; and several distinct cultures.

Preceding Pages: The San Francisco Peaks, near Flagstaff, in the fall. The peaks include Mount Humphreys, with an elevation of 12,670 feet, Arizona's highest mountain.
PHOTO BY DICK DIETRICH

Right: The Superstition Mountains in Central Arizona. Somewhere within this mountain range await the riches of the legendary Lost Dutchman's Gold Mine.
PHOTO BY JERRY JACKA

CLIMATE...

A great range in temperatures can be found throughout the state of Arizona from season to season, and often, even on the same day from region to region. Highs of 127°F have been recorded in the desert region during summer months and lows of -40°F have been reached during the winter in the mountains. Maverick, in the White Mountains, is consistently the coldest place while Yuma and Lake Havasu City along the Colorado River compete to record the highest temperatures.

Because of the low humidity, great variations in temperatures between day and night exist. The normally cloudless skies in the desert do little to deflect daytime heat but, conversely, a lack of clouds allows heat to rapidly dissipate bringing welcome relief from the day's high temperatures.

Since the elevation of the state varies so greatly from region to region, rainfall patterns are erratic. Spring is normally the driest time of year as Pacific Ocean storms move north and California's mountain capture a majority of rainfall moving to the east. Arizona has two rainy seasons– winter, when Pacific storms are further south and the smaller mountains of Southern California provide less of a barrier; and summer, when the high winds (between 10,000 and 20,000 feet) shift from the west to the southeast.

Summer months provide Arizona's heaviest rainfall as "monsoon" season arrives from the Gulf of Mexico. During afternoon cloudbursts several inches of rain may fall in a few minutes as spectacular lightning storms occur. The monsoons, though welcomed by locals, often cause considerable damage as torrents rush through dry creek beds and washes.

In early fall another kind of storm occurs in Arizona as tropical moisture arrives from the Gulf of California or the Gulf of Mexico and the upper air shifts from the southeast to the west and tropical rains fall. Unlike the monsoons, these rains fall during the day or night instead of primarily during the afternoon.

TEMPERATURES AND RAINFALL

With elevations varying from 138 feet above sea level in Yuma, to 12,670 feet in the San Francisco Peaks, Arizona has a varied climate– from dry desert to Arctic-alpine.

Area	Elevation In Feet	Average Summer Temperatures	Average Winter Temperatures	Average Annual Rainfall in Inches
Alpine	8000	77°-40°	47°-11°	20.7
Casa Grande	1405	105°-71°	68°-35°	8.2
Cottonwood	3320	96°-66°	59°-32°	10.1
Douglas	3973	94-64°	69°-31°	12.2
Flagstaff	6903	78°-47°	42°-16°	20.3
Gila Bend	737	107°-73°	70°-38°	5.7
Grand Canyon	6968	82°-51°	43°-20°	15.8
Kingman	3333	95°-63°	58°-32°	10.6
McNary	7320	79°-45°	45°-18°	24.7
Nogales	3800	94°-62°	65°-31°	15.6
Parker	425	106°-73°	65°-31°	4.8
Phoenix	1083	102°-74°	67°-41°	7.7
Prescott	5410	87°-53°	52°-21°	19.3
Snowflake	5644	89°-52°	50°-18°	12.2
Tombstone	4540	92°-64°	61°-35°	14.1
Tucson	2410	99°-69°	66°-36°	10.9
Wickenburg	2070	100°-65°	65°-31°	11.0
Yuma	138	104°-74°	69°-44°	3.4

Source: Institute of Atmospheric Physics, The University of Arizona, Tucson.

THE SEVEN LIFE ZONES

In the study of ecology, the science dealing with all living things, seven life zones have been established between the Equator and the North Pole. The study of life zones was formulated by Clinton Hart Merriam, one of the world's great naturalists, for the U.S. Department of Agriculture in the late 1800s and early 1900s.

Traveling through Arizona, from the lower elevations of the drier desert regions to the higher elevations of towering mountain peaks, visitors pass through all seven life zones, the equivalent of a trip from the Equator to the North Pole.

Merriam concluded changes in elevation of 1000 feet will have basically the same effect on plant and animal life as changes of 300-500 miles in latitude. He also determined temperatures will drop between 3 and 5 degrees for each 1000 foot rise in elevation.

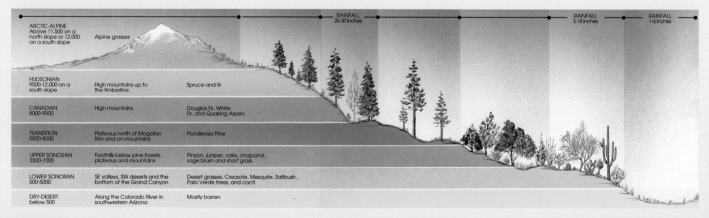

ARCTIC-ALPINE Above 11,500 on a north slope or 12,000 on a south slope	Alpine grasses	
HUDSONIAN 9500-12,000 on a south slope	High mountains up to the timberline	Spruce and fir
CANADIAN 8000-9500	High mountains	Douglas Fir, White Fir, and Quaking Aspen
TRANSITION 5500-8500	Plateaus north of Mogollon Rim and on mountains	Ponderosa Pine
UPPER SONORAN 3500-7000	Foothills below pine forests, plateaus and mountains	Pinyon, juniper, oaks, chaparral, sage brush and short grass
LOWER SONORAN 500-5000	SE valleys, SW deserts and the bottom of the Grand Canyon	Desert grasses, Creosote, Mesquite, Saltbush, Palo Verde trees, and cacti
DRY-DESERT below 500	Along the Colorado River in southwestern Arizona	Mostly barren

RAINFALL 25-30 inches

RAINFALL 3-18 inches

RAINFALL 1-6 inches

PARKS AND MONUMENTS...

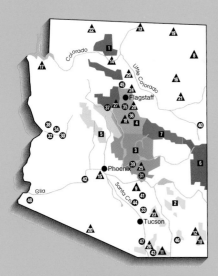

NATIONAL FOREST

Apache Coconino Coronado Kaibab

Prescott Sitgreaves Tonto

■ National Forests

1 Kaibab National Forest
2 Coronado National Forest
3 Tonto National Forest
4 Coconino National Forest
5 Prescott National Forest
6 Apache National Forest
7 Sitgreaves National Forest

▲ Arizona's National Parks and Monuments

8 Canyon de Chelly National Monument
9 Casa Grande Ruins National Monument
10 Chiricahua National Monument
11 Coronado National Memorial
12 Fort Bowie National Historic Site
13 Glen Canyon National Recreation Area
14 Grand Canyon National Park
15 Hohokam Pima National Monument
16 Hubbell Trading Post National Historic Site
17 Lake Mead National Recreational Area
18 Montezuma Castle National Monument
19 Navajo National Monument
20 Organ Pipe Cactus National Monument
21 Petrified Forest National Park
22 Pipe Spring National Monument
23 Saguaro National Monument
24 Sunset Crater Volcano National Monument
25 Tonto National Monument
26 Tumacacori National Historical Park
27 Tuzigoot National Monument
28 Walnut Canyon National Monument
29 Wupatki National Monument

● Arizona State Parks

30 Alamo Lake
31 Boyce Thompson Arboretum
32 Buckskin Mountain
33 Catalina
34 Cattail Cove
35 Dead Horse Ranch

36 Fort Verde
37 Jerome
38 Lake Havasu
39 Lost Dutchman
40 Lyman Lake
41 McFarland Historic
42 Painted Rock
43 Patagonia Lake
44 Picacho Peak
45 Riordan Historic
46 Tombstone Courthouse
47 Tubac Presidio
48 Yuma Territorial Prison

Above: Kaibab National Forest in fall.
PHOTO BY CHARLES CHANLEY

ARIZONA INDIAN RESERVATION POPULATIONS

Reservation	Classification	Population
Ak-Chin	Papago-Pima	389
Camp Verde	Yavapai-Apache	521
Cocopah	Cocopah	835
Colorado River	Mohave-Chemehuevi	2,070*
Fort Apache	Apache	8,100
Fort McDowell	Yavapai	348
Fort Mojave	Mojave	700*
Fort Yuma	Quechan	1,500
Gila River	Pima-Maricopa	9,404
Havasupai	Havasupai	475
Hopi	Hopi	8,253
Hualapai	Hualapai	1,133
Kaibab-Paiute	Paiute	224
Navajo	Navajo	83,000±
Papago	Papago	16,307+
Pascua Yaqui	Pascua Yaqui	4,772
Salt River	Pima-Maricopa	3,313
San Carlos	Apache	6,090
Tonto Apache	Tonto Apache	67
Yavapai-Prescott	Yavapai	73

Note: Figures are supplied by the Bureau of Indian Affairs and the Navajo Nation, and are for Arizona only.

KAIBAB	NAJAVO	FT. APACHE	HUALAPAI	GILA
PAPAGO	HAVASUPAI	HOPI	ZUNI	SAN CARLOS
FT. McDOWELL	SALT RIVER	AK-CHIN	COLORADO RIVER	SAN XAVIER
MOHAVE	GILA BEND	COCOPAH	PASCUA YAQUI	

*These population figures include California for the Colorado River, Fort Mojave and Fort Yuma reservations.
±Total Navajo population is approximately 160,000.
+Papago figures include Sells (11,307), Gila Bend (703) and San Xavier (4665).

THE GRAND CANYON

"Long ago there was a great wise chief, who mourned the death of his wife and would not be comforted until Ta-vwoats, one of the Indian gods, came to him and told him she was in a happier land, and offered to take him there, that he might see for himself, if, upon his return, he would cease to mourn. The great chief promised. Then Ta-vwoats made a trail through the mountains that intervene between that beautiful land, the balmy region in the great west, and this, the desert home of the poor Nu'-ma.

This trail was the canyon gorge of the Colorado. Through it he led him and, when they had returned, the deity had exacted from the chief a promise that he would tell no one of the great joys of that land, lest, through discontent with the circumstances of this world, they should desire to go to heaven. Then he rolled a river into the gorge, a mad, raging stream, that should engulf any that might attempt to enter thereby.

More than once have I been warned by the Indians not to enter this canyon. They consider it disobedience to the gods and contempt for their authority, and believed that it would surely bring upon me their wrath."

–John Wesley Powell, 1869

Exploration of the Grand Canyon by the Europeans began on a less than auspicious note. In fact, the first explorers in the region found it to be of little economic value. In 1540, Spanish conquistador, Francisco Vasques de Coronado, led the first European expedition through the territory then known as New Spain, along a route that is currently through parts of Arizona, New Mexico, Texas, Oklahoma and Kansas.

Coronado, along with 336 Spaniards; 1,000 Indian allies; 1,500 horses and mules; and numerous sheep and cattle, was in search of the legendary Seven Cities of Cibola, also called the "Seven Cities of Gold." On August 25, 1540, Coronado sent 25 men, commanded by Captain Garcia Lopez de Cardenas, north to the Colorado Plateau to investigate stories of a great river and a people who possessed great wealth. Cardenas and his party arrived at the edge of the Grand Canyon, probably in an area along the South Rim, and found neither the gold they were seeking nor the route to the river below. Disappointed, they neglected to even name the giant abyss.

Following attempts to locate sources of the great wealth earlier explorers had been able to loot from the South and Central American cultures proved futile and Spanish exploration passed from the hands of the conquistadors to the Spanish Franciscan missionaries. The Franciscans retained an interest in the region, although it was more than 200 years before the next Spaniard, Father Francisco Garces, gave the Canyon its first European name, Puerto de Bucareli, or "Bucareli Pass," in honor of Antonio Maria de Bucareli y Ursua, who was then Viceroy of New Spain.

During the 1820's, American fur trappers may have traveled through the Grand Canyon in search of Beaver pelts, although there is no written record to substantiate their presence. In 1821, Mexico gained independence from Spain and control of New Spain, including Arizona, passed to Mexican hands for a period lasting 27 years.

The signing of the Treaty of Guadalupe Hidalgo, in 1848, ended the war between Mexico and the United States and the region became a territory of the United States. These two rapid changes in ownership did little to promote exploration of the region until, for political reasons, President James Buchanan called for surveys to the area in 1857.

President Buchanan ordered troops to Utah as friction developed between the United States and Mormons in Utah and northern Arizona. Buchanan felt there was a strong possibility the Mormons were in a state of open rebellion and ordered the army to the area to ensure federal control.

Searching for a supply route into Utah from the south, Lieutenant Joseph Christmas Ives of the Corps of Topical Engineers was sent to find the northernmost point of steamship navigation possible on the Colorado River.

Left: Rain clouds above the Grand Canyon from Mather Point. Stephen Tyng Mather (1867-1930) was the National Park Service's first director.
PHOTO BY JERRY JACKA

Right: Hopi Point at sunrise. The Colorado River is visible in the background.
PHOTO BY JERRY SIEVE

Ives established this point at Black Canyon, where he ran hard aground. He then traveled east to Peach Springs Canyon where he, along with members of his expedition, descended into the canyon and followed Diamond Creek north to the Colorado River. The expedition arrived at the Grand Canyon in April of 1858.

Mouth of Black Canyon in a drawing from the 1857 expedition of Lt. Joseph Christmas Ives.

After cursory examination of the area, Ives continued his journey to Fort Defiance, in eastern Arizona, where he entered his report and concluded the Grand Canyon was valueless, much the same as his Spanish predecessors had centuries before. In fact, Ives stated in his official report, "Ours has been the first, and will doubtless be the last, party of whites to visit this profitless locality."

Dr. John Strong Newberry was the geologist for the 1857 expedition Lieutenant Ives.
PHOTO COURTESY GRAND CANYON NATIONAL PARK

Although Lieutenant Ives found little economic or strategic value to the Grand Canyon, which had been his assigned task, accompanying him on the expedition was Dr. John Strong Newberry, who, in his written reports, became the first white man to ever ponder the Canyon and question its geological formation. Dr. Newberry wrote of the physical features of the canyons, rocks and fossils he observed and concluded that the river itself had eroded the canyons. His reports were the first by an academic to describe the natural wonders and the beauty of the Grand Canyon.

During the decade following Ives' expedition small groups of prospectors roamed through the Canyon in search of mineral deposits. Like the conquistadors before them, it is possible their quest for material wealth kept them from noticing the natural beauty of the area.

In 1869, John Wesley Powell, a one-armed former Union Army major, undertook a bold and imaginative expedition to prove that it was possible to navigate the Colorado River by boat along its entire canyon passages. The major's well written accounts fired readers imaginations and was a key factor in developing the continuing interest in the Grand Canyon.

John Wesley Powell.
PHOTO COURTESY GRAND CANYON NATIONAL PARK. IDENTIFICATION NUMBER 5133.

Major Powell and his associates explored northern areas of the Colorado Plateau in 1870 while planning a second expedition down the Colorado River. During spring of 1871, Major Powell was sent by the federal government to map the Colorado Plateau and the Colorado River. Far more time was spent on this second expedition and attention was focused on exploration of both sides of the river and surveying the canyon areas.

The accounts of Major Powell's explorations were first published in 1874, and soon gained a large readership in the United States and, after translation to foreign languages, were widely read throughout Europe. His was the first of thousands of Colorado River trips by made by adventurers from around the world.

Clarence Edward Dutton, a protege of Major Powell's, led the first geological expedition of the Grand Canyon in 1880. Dutton continued in-depth studies of the Canyon and wrote the first volume on the Canyon's geology.

Clarence Dutton's book contained illustrations by Thomas Moran, an Englishman who had previously illustrated the area while serving as an artist on the second expedition of Major Powell. Moran was not a member of the boat expedition down the Canyon and had

President Benjamin Harrison designated the Grand Canyon a forest reserve in 1893.
COURTESY NATIONAL ARCHIVES

to create his drawings from photographs taken by the expedition's photographer. Dutton, along with Major Powell, concluded that the Colorado River was older than the landforms it flowed through. They both felt, erroneously, that prior to the formation of the Canyon as we find it today, the river had cut its way deeper and deeper into the formations it flowed through as time passed.

Throughout the late 1880's, interest in the Canyon continued to build. In 1882 and 1883, and again during 1886, Benjamin Harrison, a senator from Indiana, introduced bills hoping to establish the Grand Canyon as a national park. Even though he was unsuccessful, he was able to designate the area as the Grand Canyon Forest Reserve in 1893 after he was elected President of the United States. President

President Woodrow Wilson signed the bill creating Grand Canyon National Park in 1919.
COURTESY NATIONAL ARCHIVES

Harrison's actions prevented the seizure of land by settlers. In 1908, establishment of the

Grand Canyon National Monument ensured a ban on prospecting and mining, and finally, on February 26, 1919, President Woodrow Wilson signed a bill creating Grand Canyon National Park. Today, more than four million people visit the Grand Canyon each year.

Thomas Moran sketching the Canyon. Powell's report, *The Exploration of the Colorado River of the West*, included 29 Moran illustrations.

JOHN WESLEY POWELL'S GRAND CANYON EXPLORATIONS

On May 24, 1869, Major John Wesley Powell, a retired Union Army officer who had lost his right arm during the Civil War at the Battle of Shiloh, set out to travel the length of the Colorado River through the Grand Canyon by boat. Major Powell, who had a background in the study of natural sciences and a particular interest in the field of geology, embarked on his famous journey from Green River, Wyoming.

Green River was chosen because it was a stop on the Union Pacific Railroad, which had reached the area a few years before. With a railhead, the pine boats and supplies needed for the expedition could easily be delivered to its starting point.

Major Powell descended the Green River to the Colorado River with nine men in four pine boats. On the first leg of the journey, one boat was destroyed and one expedition member declared that he had seen enough danger and quit.

The remaining members of Powell's expedition continued down the Colorado through Cataract Canyon, Glen Canyon and finally entered the Grand Canyon. While in the Grand Canyon, at what is now called Separation Rapid, three more men decided it was unsafe to continue and left the river to find an overland route to safety. This proved to be an unwise decision, for the three men were never seen again. At the end of the journey Major Powell sat in camp with his journal and wrote, "Now the danger is over; now the toil has ceased; now the gloom has disappeared; and what a vast expanse of constellations can be seen! The river rolls by us in silent majesty;

Above: Two of the pine river boats of Powell's second expedition near the upper end of the Grand Canyon in 1872.
PHOTO COURTESY GRAND CANYON NATIONAL PARK.
IDENTIFICATION NUMBER 5309

the quiet of the camp is sweet; our joy is almost ecstasy. We sit till long after mid-night, talking of the Grand Canyon, talking of home, but chiefly talking of the three men who left us. Are they wandering in those depths, unable to find a way out? Are they searching over the desert land above for water? Are they nearing settlements?"

Major Powell and his party, who had explored 1048 miles in 98 days, did not yet realize the three missing men would never be found. As time went by, the general consensus was that they were probably killed by a band of Paiute Indians living in the Grand Canyon area. No trace of their remains has ever been found.

Right: Map tracing Powell's first river expedition from Green River through Cataract Canyon, Glen Canyon and the Grand Canyon.

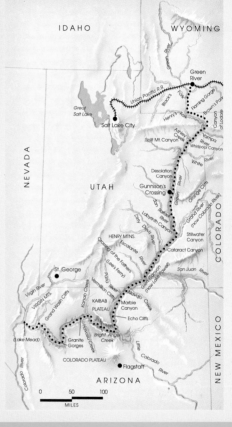

Early Development of the Grand Canyon...

In 1884, William Wallace Bass established a camp near Havasupai Point, 27 miles west of the present site of Grand Canyon Village. His only competition for tourist accommodations was the Farlee Hotel, a one-room shanty, that opened the same year at the junction of Peach Springs Canyon and Diamond Creek.

In 1886, John Hance, the first white settler on the South Rim, offered lodging at his ranch near Grandview Point. Hance was a colorful character who continued to offer his services as a guide and tour operator at the Canyon until his death in 1919. Known for telling tall tales, Hance once said, when asked about the missing tip of one of his fingers, that he had worn it off pointing at the Grand Canyon.

In 1896, J. Wilbur Thurber purchased John Hance's hotel. Thurber started construction on the Bright Angel Hotel in Grand Canyon

Construction on the Bright Angel Hotel in Grand Canyon Village began in 1897.
PHOTO COURTESY GRAND CANYON NATIONAL PARK I.D. NO.3494

The Grandview Hotel, opened in 1897, was the first hotel to be located on the Canyon's rim.
PHOTO COURTESY GRAND CANYON NATIONAL PARK IDENTIFICATION NUMBER 990

John D. Lee and the Mountain Meadows Massacre

Lees Ferry, founded in 1869 by John Doyle Lee, a Mormon with seventeen wives, was a quiet spot that offered the only feasible place to cross the Colorado River in this northern region of Arizona. The town's remote location provided a tranquil setting until 1877, when the heinous crimes of its founder's past rocked the small community to its foundation.

During the 1850s, Utah's Mormon population had a reputation throughout much of the rest of the country for zealotry and fanaticism. Tempers often ran high between Mormons and non-Mormons, with the exception of the local Indians, who were the Mormons only allies. Under the leadership of Brigham Young, the Mormons lived in relative peace with their Indian neighbors. They believed the Indians were brothers– "through the loins of Joseph and Manassah"– who had fallen from grace. This, the Mormons felt, was evidenced by their dark skin. The alliance between Mormons and Indians laid the groundwork for the nefarious incident that became known as the Mountain Meadows Massacre.

In 1857, the Fancher Party, emigrants from Arkansas and Missouri, drove their wagon train and 300 head of cattle through southern Utah bound for California. They made the tactless mistake of shouting insults at the Mormons and naming one of their oxen Brigham Young. One member of the wagon train boasted that the pistol he carried was the one used to kill the Mormon's martyred leader, Joseph Smith.

During this same time, the Mormons were already incensed upon learning that federal troops, under the direction of President James A. Buchanan, were en route to Utah from the east. The emigrants, prodded in part by a group of rowdy Missourians in their party, made the fatal mistake of threatening to return with an armed force once they reached California. This proved to be a tragically unfortunate boast.

The Mormons, under the leadership of Lee, who had previously been in charge of Indian affairs in southern Utah, were still smarting from the insults and years of injustices in their previous homes in Illinois, Ohio and Missouri. Any reference to the martyrdom of Joseph Smith was more than they could bear, especially by anyone from Missouri.

Under a white flag of truce, Lee and 54 Mormon militiamen approached the Fancher Party, offering to provide safe passage through a territory rife with hostile Indians. As soon as the emigrants had accepted the Mormon offer and laid down their weapons, the militiamen opened fire upon the men, cutting them down where they stood. The Indians, who were allies of the Mormons, stormed the wagon train and slaughtered the women and all of the older children. When the bloodbath ended, only seventeen children, all too young to recount the incident, were alive.

For the next 20 years the community closed ranks and refused to assist the federal government in prosecuting the guilty parties. Lee fled the area and settled in the remote region that became Lees Ferry. Feeling secure in his isolation, he built the original ferry in 1872. He was only able to operate his enterprise, which continued until the Navajo Bridge was built in 1929, for a short period.

In 1875, Lee was arrested and tried for his part in the Mountain Meadows Massacre. His first trial resulted in a hung jury and he was sentenced to a lifetime in prison. After serving two years of his sentence, he was granted a new trial and released for a few months on bail. In 1877, he was again tried for his part in the massacre, the only Mormon ever tried for the grisly incident, and was convicted.

Lee accompanied his captors to Mountain Meadows where, as he sat blindfolded on the coffin that was to hold his remains, he was executed by firing squad.

John Doyle Lee, founder of Lees Ferry, was the only person brought to trial for the Mountain Meadows Massacre.
COURTESY ARIZONA HISTORICAL SOCIETY

Village during the following year. John Hance became the first postmaster at the Canyon, which was then called Tourist, Arizona. In 1897, the Grandview Hotel opened its doors on the South Rim and became the first hotel to be located on the Canyon's rim.

Transportation to the Canyon took on new dimensions as the 20th century unfurled. In 1901, the first scheduled passenger train arrived and the Bright Angel Hotel was bought by Martin Buggeln. 1902, the first automobiles arrived and the tourist boom was on. Emory and Ellsworth Kolb established a photography studio at Grand Canyon Village, in 1903, and Ralph H. Cameron, who later became a United States Senator, opened the Cameron Hotel. The same year, President Theodore Roosevelt first visited the Canyon and became enraptured with its beauty. President Roosevelt was responsible for preserving the Grand Canyon as Grand Canyon National Monument in 1908.

In 1904, the El Tovar Hotel was built by the Fred Harvey Company, who, in 1906, bought the Bright Angel Hotel from Martin Buggeln.

William Wallace Bass opened the first school at the Grand Canyon, in 1911, and the following year Arizona became the nation's 48th state. In 1914, Hermit's Rest was designed by Mary Elizabeth Jane Colter, the famous Fred Harvey Company architect.

Ellsworth and Emory Kolb in 1903.
PHOTO COURTESY NORTHERN ARIZONA UNIVERSITY

Preceding pages: A modern day explorer navigates the Colorado River through Marble Canyon.
PHOTO BY JIM COWLIN

Right: Double rainbows over the Grand Canyon from Desert View.
PHOTO BY CHARLES CHANLEY

GEOLOGY

Arizona has been shaped by the ravages of the forces of nature and the passage of time. The land was once covered by seas. Rivers cut deep gorges through surface stratas and earthquakes bent, twisted and dropped the land. Volcanoes erupted and the land suffered innumerable droughts. If these events had all occurred at the same time, Arizona would surely have been hell on earth, or a perfect sound stage for a Steven Spielberg movie. Fortunately these forces occurred over the past four billion years, not overnight.

There is no better place in the world to study the earth's formation the Grand Canyon. From Canyon rims visitors gaze down at as much as 6,250 feet of geological history, more than is exposed anywhere else on the planet.

In the millions of years the Colorado River has carved its way through the formations of the Canyon it has exposed a fossil record dating to the first living organisms. The earliest fossils imprinted in the rock are of sea life resembling jellyfish. In higher layers of the Canyon walls fossils remain from the earth's earliest days.

Geologists divide the earth's history into past eras– Precambrian, all geologic time up to 600 million years ago; Paleozoic, 600 million to 225 million years ago; Mesozoic, 225 million to 65 million years ago; and Cenozoic, the last 65 million years. Eras are divided into periods and periods into epochs.

During the Precambrian Era, Arizona was covered by seas. Land gradually formed as shallow seas advanced and retreated, leaving thousands of feet of silt and mud behind. Lava flows created mountains. At least twice during Precambrian times, earthquakes twisted and folded the land into mountain ranges at least twice as tall as those visible today.

During the Paleozoic Era the region remained under water for millions of years. Two large islands remained above sea level– an area that today is Window Rock and a high spot near Yuma. The seas left sediments that formed sandstone, shale and limestone in formations easily viewed in Canyon de Chelly and Oak Creek Canyon. Limestone forming the rims of the Grand Canyon was deposited during the Paleozoic Era.

The Mesozoic Era is also known as the age of the dinosaurs. Fossils of these prehistoric creatures have been found throughout the state. Copper deposits, left by retreating seas, and the Petrified Forest were created during the Mesozoic Era. Near the end of the era, rain and streams eroded materials containing uranium and vast coal deposits were left by a sea that had entered from the north.

In the Cenozoic Era, the Rocky Mountains rose to the northeast of Arizona. Widespread faulting occurred and the earth was bent, folded and cracked. Around 30 million years ago, the Colorado Plateau was raised to its present height and the last volcanic eruptions occurred.

The illustration above, by English artist Thomas Moran, is one of several made to depict Major John Wesley Powell's exploration of the Grand Canyon. Moran's excellent drawings played and important part in creating interest in the text of Major Powell's now historic report on the exploration of the Colorado River.

Preceding Pages: Sunset at Mather Point on the South Rim of the Grand Canyon. Exposed formations of the Canyon's walls display the last 1.7 billion years of earth's geological history.
PHOTO BY JERRY JACKA

Left: Brahma Temple catches the sun's last rays at Bright Angel Point on the North Rim of the Grand Canyon.
PHOTO BY BOB CLEMENZ

Right: The Canyon walls at Toroweap Point frame Lava Falls on the Colorado River.
PHOTO BY BOB CLEMENZ

ROCK NAME

Rock Name	THICKNESS (In Feet)	DEPOSITIONAL ENVIRONMENT	AGE (millions of years)	Era	Period
KAIBAB LIMESTONE	300-500	SEA	250		Middle Permian
TOROWEAP FORMATION	250-450	SEA	260		Middle Permian
COCONINO SANDSTONE	50-350	DESERT	270		Early Permian
HERMIT SHALE	250-1,000	FLOODPLAIN	280		Early Permian
SUPAI GROUP	950-1,350	SWAMP	300	PALEOZOIC	Early Permian / Pennsylvanian
REDWALL LIMESTONE	450-700	SEA	330		Early and Middle Mississippian
	30-1,000	SEA	370		Late Devonian
TEMPE BUTTE LIMESTONE	DISCONFORMITY		400-500		Silurian and Orodovician
MUAV LIMESTONE	50-1,000	SEA	530		Middle Cambrian
BRIGHT ANGEL SHALE	200-450	SEA	540		Early and Middle Cambrian
TAPEATS SANDSTONE	100-300	SEA	550		Early Cambrian
	THE GREAT UNCONFORMITY		570-800		
GRAND CANYON SUPERGROUP	15,000	SEA	800-1,200	PRECAMBRIAN	Late
VISHNU SCHIST		Metamorphosed Sea Sediments	1,700		Early
ZOROASTER GRANITE		Molten Intrusion			

VISHNU SCHIST

SEQUENCE OF EXPOSED ROCK FORMATIONS

NORTH • KAIBAB·PLATEAU • NORTH RIM • SOUTH RIM • GRAND CANYON • COCONINO PLATEAU • MESA BUTTE FAULT • SAN FRANCISCO PEAKS • SOUTH

GEOLOGIC CROSS SECTION OF THE GRAND CANYON REGION

Although the epic production that created the Grand Canyon began more than 2 billion years ago, the last 4 million years has shown the most significant changes to the surface topography.

2 billion years ago: Volcanic materials and sediments accumulated.

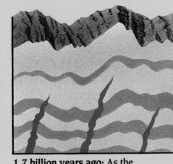

1.7 billion years ago: As the mountains were uplifted, rocks metamorphosed into Vishnu Schist.

1.5 billion years ago: Erosion brought the mountains to a nearly level plain.

1.2 billion years ago: As the plain subsided the Grand Canyon Supergroup layers were deposited.

800 million years ago: Fault block mountains were formed.

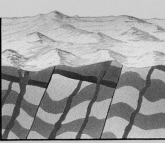

700 million years ago: The fault block mountains eroded into hilly topography.

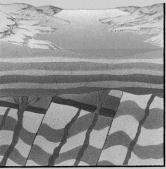

600 million years ago: The area subsided and Paleozoic layers were deposited.

230 million years ago: Mesozoic sediments were deposited.

65 million years ago: Faulting activity uplifted the Mesozoic.

4 million years ago: The Colorado River began to cut its path.

These ten major, large scale geological events worked together, over the last 2 billion years, to form what is the Grand Canyon today. The actual date each event occurred can only be approximated by the evidence found in the exposed rocks of the canyon's walls.

Below: The Colorado River surges through House Rock Rapids in Marble Canyon.
PHOTO BY JIM COWLIN

The Havasupai have inhabited the lush confines of Havasu Canyon since long before the first Europeans arrived in the Americas. A peaceful agrarian people, the Havasupai share the splendor of their canyon with a variety of flora and fauna and have always welcomed visitors fit enough to reach their domain.

Havasu Canyon has often been described as Shangri-la, Utopia, Paradise and countless other glowing phrases that depict a surreal, heavenly environment. Words, nor photographs, alone cannot describe the inspiring beauty of this secluded oasis.

Located along the southwestern border of Grand Canyon National Park, Havasu Canyon offers a stunning contrast to the barren terrain of the plateau above. Nearly 3,000 feet below the trailhead at Hualapai Hilltop on the plateau above, Havasu Canyon is a lush, semi-tropical wonderland where a variety of flora, fauna, and the Havasupai people, enjoy the bounty of an idyllic streamside community.

Havasu Creek flows through the canyon's gorge, its clear, spring-fed waters in striking contrast to the neighboring Colorado River which is quite often laden with silt. The creek emerges from natural springs and– as its mineral-laden waters journey through the red rock limestone walled canyon, plunging over precipitous cliffs creating numerous waterfalls– the minerals in the waters leave deposits of travertine, creating small dams and striking blue-green pools. These pools provide water for the riparian community along their banks and inspiration to those fortunate enough to have journeyed to the canyon's depths.

Havasu Canyon has been home to Native Americans for more than 1,000 years. The Havasupai, whose name means "the people that live where the waters are blue-green," inherited the canyon from earlier residents.

The village of Supai, deep within the towering walls of Havasu Canyon, is a secluded setting of remarkable beauty.

The first written record of the Havasupai dates to 1776, when Father Francisco Garces, a Spanish missionary, visited the area. For the next century there was little contact with Europeans, except for determined trappers and prospectors who visited the area. Always a peaceful people, the Havasupai are warm and friendly and have always enjoyed visitors to their remote location.

Throughout the centuries their existence has depended on farming the lush and fertile lands of Havasu Canyon. They supplemented their diets in the past by hunting game animals, and today, they raise livestock. Corn, squash and beans are their staples. Their fruit crops consist of peaches, nectarines, apricots and figs. The peaches are said to have been introduced to the Havasupai, in the late 1850s, by John Doyle Lee, a Mormon fugitive who lived among these people for several years following the Mountain Meadows Massacre.

Around a mile-and-a-half downstream from Supai is Navajo Falls, which was named after a famous Havasupai chief. Havasu Falls is located two miles downstream from the village and although not tremendously high, at just under 100 feet, is known throughout the world for its beauty and the travertine dams formed in the pool below. The highest waterfall within Havasu Canyon, at approximately 196 feet, is Mooney Falls.

Preceding pages: Sundown in winter at Hopi Point. Hopi Point was named for the Hopi people of northern Arizona, whose name translates as "the peaceful people."
PHOTO BY JERRY SIEVE

Left: Havasu Falls, with a plunge of nearly 100 feet, is among the most beautiful waterfalls in the world. Below the falls the blue-green waters of Havasu Creek flow over travertine dams.
PHOTO BY CHARLES CHANLEY

Right: Havasu Creek cascades over a series of natural travertine dams. The dams are formed as mineral laden creek water leaves deposits of travertine, a cream-colored limestone that is mostly calcium carbonate.
PHOTO BY STEVE BRUNO

Below: Beaver Falls, named for the large aquatic rodents, *Castor canadensis*, calling the area home, is a series of cascades and falls in the twenty to thirty foot range that produce a number of large turquoise pools.
PHOTO BY STEVE BRUNO

Right: Mooney Falls was named for prospector James Mooney who fell to his death near the falls in 1880. At approximately 196 feet, Mooney Falls is the highest waterfall in Havasu Canyon.
PHOTO BY CHARLES CHANLEY

Right: Angel's Window, on the North Rim near Cape Royal, is a large natural arch framing the Grand Canyon beyond.
PHOTO BY BOB CLEMENZ

Left: A winter afternoon at Mather Point at the South Rim of the Grand Canyon. Bright Angel Canyon, seen below the rim, is home to Bright Angel Creek. The creek has cut a path through this side canyon in a straight line that is nearly eleven miles in length.
PHOTO BY JERRY SIEVE

Following pages: A view of Mount Hayden from Point Imperial on the North Rim. Mount Hayden, formed of Coconino Sandstone, was named for Arizona pioneer Charles Trumbull Hayden, the founder of the city of Tempe.
PHOTO BY DICK DIETRICH

WILDLIFE

Few areas in the world offer a greater variety of wildlife species than can be found in Arizona. The state has a broad assortment of mammals, birds, fish, reptiles and amphibians. More than 60 percent of all wildlife species found in North America are found within Arizona's borders.

The state's seven life zones provide a diverse range of habitats– from the Dry Desert Zone, with elevations below 500 feet above sea level– to the Arctic-Alpine Zone, found in elevations above 11,500 feet. More than 3,500 plant species provide food and shelter for a diverse animal population spread through the state.

Arizona has nine species of large mammals including: Elk, *Cervus canadensis*, which are sometimes referred to as Wapiti; Pronghorn, *Antilocapra americana;* Mule Deer, *Odocoileus hemionus;* Whitetail Deer, *Odocoileus virginianus;* Black Bear, *Ursus americanus;* Javalina, *Pecari angulatus;* Bighorn, *Ovis canadensis;* Bison, *Bison bison;* and Mountain Lion, *Felis concolor,* which are also referred to as Panther, Cougar, Puma, Painter and Catamount. Elk, the largest mammals found in the state, are mainly seen in the Apache, Coconino, Sitgreave and Tonto national forests. Pronghorn and deer are found throughout the state, although they are most common in northern and central areas.

Of a more dangerous note, Arizona once had two species of bear– Black Bear and Grizzly Bear, *Ursus horribilis,* a name that translate from the Latin as "horrible bear." The last of the Grizzly Bears is commonly thought to have been killed in the White Mountains in 1916. The Black Bear is still a fairly common sight in the mountain regions of the state.

Mountain Lions are another predator found mainly in the mountain regions although they have been observed on many occasions in the Sonoran Desert. A member of the cat family, Mountain Lions reach a length of four feet and adults can weigh more than 125 lbs. They prey on Elk, deer, Pronghorn, Javelina and smaller mammals. On occasion Mountain Lions take domestic livestock– an unfortunate habit which has caused ranchers to severely limit their populations. There are no records of Mountain Lion attacks on humans in Arizona.

Smaller mammals include Badger, *Taxidea Taxus;* Bobcat, *Lynx rufus;* Raccoon, *Procyon lotor;* Coyote, *Canis latrans;* Ringtail, *Bassariscus astutus;* Porcupine, *Erethizon dorsatum;* Gray Fox, *Urocyon cinereoargenteus;* Stripped Skunk, *Mephitis mephitis;* Spotted Skunk, *Spilogale putorius;* Desert Cottontail, *Sylvilagus auduboni;* and Jackrabbit, *Lepus americanus.* Beaver, *Castor canadensis,* are found along streams.

More than 300 species of birds call Arizona home. The smallest are hummingbirds and the largest is the Merriam Wild Turkey. Three species of quail and two migratory doves are found in abundant quantities throughout the state. Turkey Vulture, Red-tailed Hawk, Harris Hawk, Roadrunner, Great Horned Owl, Raven, Woodpecker, Purple Martin, Boat-tailed Grackle, Cactus Wren, Bluebird, Great Blue Heron, Snowy Egret and Cardinal are common sights.

More than 750 species of birds, mammals, reptiles, amphibians and fish are native to Arizona including four species of squirrels– the Abert, Kaibab, Arizona Gray and Red.

Left: Rocky Mountain Mule Deer doe, *Odocoileus hemionus*, at the Grand Canyon's North Rim.
PHOTO BY JAMES TALLON

Right: Great Blue Heron, *Ardea herodias*, nest singly or in colonies, along streams and lakes throughout Arizona.
PHOTO BY JAMES TALLON

Yellow-Pine Woodland Community...

The Yellow-Pine Woodland Community is found between 7000 and 8200 foot elevations and contains Ponderosa Pine, Gambel Oak, Blue Elderberry and Mountain Mahogany. This biotic community is generally more open than those at higher elevations, allowing grasses and shrubs to grow on the forest's floor. Rainfall is normally in excess of twenty inches annually.

Yellow-Pine Woodlands are home to Mule Deer, Bobcat, Porcupine and to Kaibab Squirrel, found only on the North Rim of the Grand Canyon. This large white-tailed squirrel is distinctive for its ear tufts, or tassels. The Kaibab build nests high in Ponderosa Pines and feed on the inner bark and pine seeds of the trees. In summer, they may occasionally be seen feeding on mushrooms growing on the forest floor. The Kaibab closely resemble the Abert Squirrel, which also have tufted ears. Thousands of years ago, the Grand Canyon separated Kaibabs from Aberts and, in the years that followed, Kaibabs developed totally white tails while Aberts grew tails that were gray on top and white underneath.

The Yellow-Pine Woodland Community is also home to the Merriam Wild Turkey, which at times is driven down to lower elevations of the Pinyon-Juniper Woodland Community by heavy snowfall, although they prefer the

tall Ponderosa Pine for their roost sites. The Merriam Wild Turkey is polygamous. Males round up a harem of females and remain with them throughout the mating season. At this time, physiological changes occur causing the male's head to turn deep red or bright purple. When the mating urge strikes the male puffs his feathers up to nearly twice their normal size and struts, with his tail fanned out like a peacock, about the forest floor hoping to attract the attention of a female.

Below: Bighorn Sheep, *Ovis canadensis*, have been eliminated in much of their former range by hunters and through competition with domestic livestock for forage. They are currently found in only a few, well-isolated, areas.
PHOTO BY JAMES TALLON

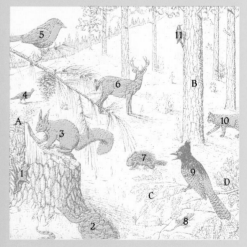

1. Deer Mouse	A. Blue Elderberry
2. Gopher Snake	B. Ponderosa Pine
3. Kaibab Squirrel	C. Gambel Oak
4. Wild Turkey	D. Mountain Mahogany
5. Western Bluebird	
6. Mule Deer	
7. Porcupine	
8. Northern Plateau Lizard	
9. Steller's Jay	
10. Bobcat	
11. Common Flicker	

Above: The Arizona Whitetail Deer, *Odocoileus virginianus*, are generally smaller than their eastern and mid-western relatives.
PHOTO BY MIKE SCULLY

32

Generally restricted to elevations above 8200 feet, the Spruce-Fir and Mountain Grassland Community consists of a mix of Blue Spruce, Aspen, White Fir, Douglas Fir and Engelmann Spruce. The high altitude of this biotic community causes cold winters, with heavy snowfalls, that allow a growing season of only a few months each year. The forest canopy is so dense few grasses or shrubs exist that are not in the meadow areas, termed Mountain Grassland Communities by biologists, scattered throughout the forest.

The Spruce-Fir Forest is home to a variety of fauna. Whitetail Deer can likely be seen in the early morning or just before the sun sets. Squirrels scamper throughout the day, along with Chipmunks and a great assortment of birds. In the evening, Bobcats travel through miles of forest in search of the small rodents that are their prey.

The Porcupine, although sometimes a meal for an aggressive Bobcat or Mountain Lion, rarely runs, or hides, from danger. At the first hint of trouble from approaching predators the Porcupine's thousands of needle-sharp quills spring to attention, making it a less-than-attractive meal for all but the most foolhardy diner. Porcupine living among the tall trees of the Spruce-Fir and Mountain Grassland communities grow to a body length of 25 inches with tails that reach 14 inches.

1. Red Squirrel
2. Mule Deer and fawn
3. Golden-mantled Ground Squirrel
4. Steller's Jay
5. Deer Mouse
6. Uinta Chipmunk
7. Western Bluebird
8. Bobcat
9. Porcupine

A. Douglas Fir
B. Kentucky Bluegrass
C. Letterman Needlegrass
D. Yarrow
E. Engelmann Spruce
F. Aspen
G. White Fir
H. Blue Spruce

Right: The Red-tailed Hawk, *Buteo jamaicensis,* is Arizona's most common large hawk. They are often seen soaring in circles above open areas.
PHOTO BY JAMES TALLON

Pinyon-Juniper Woodland Community

Sometimes referred to as the pygmy forest because of the small stature of its trees, the Pinyon-Juniper Woodland Community can be found in elevations of the Transition Zone, between 3500 and 7000 foot elevations. This biotic community occurs in the Benchlands and on the Grand Canyon's rims. Dominated by Pinyon Pine, *Pinus cembrioides,* and One-seed Juniper, *Juniperus monosperma,* Pinyon-Juniper Woodland usually shows patches of chaparral species in more open areas.

Both chaparral and woodlands are intermediate areas between desert and forest in terms of moisture, elevation and temperature. The chaparral is dominant in more arid and rocky soils, while woodlands prefer finer soils and slightly more moisture. In some areas, Arizona Oak, *Quercus arizonica,* Gambel Oak, *Quercus gambelli,* Gray Oak, *Quercus grisea,* and Emory Oak, *Quercus emoryi,* may be found along with Mormon Tea, *Ephedra viridis,* Cliffrose, *Cowania mexicana,* and Banana Yucca, *Yucca baccata.*

The Pinyon-Juniper Woodland Community is home to a variety of fauna. Desert Bighorn, may be seen in more isolated areas. Mountain Lion, the largest Arizona predators, are active at night but may at times be seen traveling their wide range in the daytime. Mule Deer are often spotted grazing at dawn or dusk.

The Curious Coatimundi

When first viewed by Spanish explorers the Coatimundi, *Nasua narica*, was mistaken for a species of monkey. This was undoubtedly caused by the Coati's habit of scurrying about with its tail held high. Equally at home in the branches of a tree or on the ground, the strange creatures are hard to categorize.

Coatimundi are exceptions to the *mammals are usually either nocturnal or crepuscular* (active at dawn or dusk) rule and can be seen during the day or night. Although they are more at home in tropical regions of Central and South America, they can easily be spotted in southern Arizona, mainly in the "island mountains" near the Mexican border. Coati have been spotted in the Phoenix Metropolitan area and as far north as the Mogollon Rim.

Traveling in troops numbering between ten and fifty members, Coatis do not seem to seek live prey, although they are omnivorous as are their relatives– the Raccoon, *Procyon lotor,* and Ringtail, *Bassariscus astutus.* Ranchers become annoyed by large numbers of Coati inhabiting their fields and groves. While crop damage is a concern, the Coati's sharply pointed canine teeth can be a problem for dogs trying to protect their master's territory. Coati often gain the advantage and dogs can be severely mauled or killed.

Right: A Coatimundi, *Nasua narica,* lounging in a tree fork. PHOTO BY JAMES TALLON

1. Sonoran Gopher Snake
2. Cliff Chipmunk
3. Short-horned Lizard
4. Desert Cottontail
5. Southern Plateau Lizard
6. Yellow-Backed Spiny Lizard
7. Gray Fox
8. Desert Bighorn
9. Mule Deer
10. Mountain Lion
11. Raven
12. Downy Woodpecker

A. Utah Juniper
B. Mormon Tea
C. Cliffrose
D. Rabbit Bush
E. Gambel Oak
F. Pinyon Pine
G. Banana Yucca

DESERT SCRUB COMMUNITY

Existing primarily in areas less than 4500 feet in elevation, the Desert Scrub Community is characterized by widely-spaced, drought resistant trees, bushes, cacti and grasses and is home to a variety of fauna able to exist in arid and semi-arid conditions.

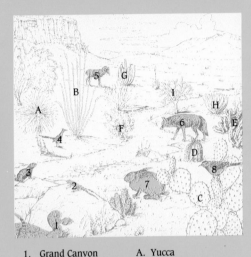

1. Grand Canyon Rattlesnake	A. Yucca
2. Chuckwalla	B. Ocotillo
3. Harris Ground Squirrel	C. Prickly Pear Cactus
4. Roadrunner	D. Barrel Cactus
5. Desert Bighorn	E. Teddy Bear Cholla
6. Coyote	F. Four-wing Saltbush
7. Jackrabbit	G. Organ Pipe Cactus
8. Cactus Wren	H. Century Plant
	I. Jumping Cholla

RIPARIAN COMMUNITY

The Riparian Community occurs along the banks of continually moist streams, lakes and rivers. These biotic communities exist along perennial or intermittent bodies of water as long as the banks remain moist enough to sustain flora and fauna relying on them.

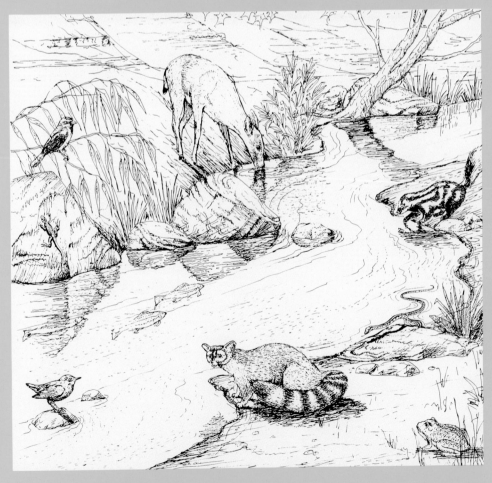

1. American Dipper	7. Wandering Garter Snake
2. Rainbow Trout	8. Rocky Mountain Toad
3. Black-throated Sparrow	9. Spotted Skunk
4. Northern Whiptail Lizard	A. Goodding Willow
5. Mule Deer	B. Arrowweed
6. Ringtail	C. Seep-willow
	D. Arizona Sycamore

CANYON DE CHELLY

Canyon de Chelly has been home to Native Americans for more than 2,000 years. The earliest records are of the Anasazi who inhabited the area until about AD 1300. They were replaced by the Hopi who were then replaced by the Navajo sometime around 1700.

anyon de Chelly, with its sheer walls and spectacularly eroded formations, has been home to Native Americans for more than 2,000 years. The first inhabitants of record were the Anasazi, a Navajo name translating roughly as "the ancient ones" or "our ancient enemies," who inhabited the area until about AD 1300. The Anasazi were replaced by the Hopi, who claim the Anasazi as ancestors, until they were themselves replaced, around 1700, by the Navajo. Canyon de Chelly today is a part of the Navajo Reservation.

More than 700 prehistoric sites are contained within the 131 square mile Canyon de Chelly National Monument. The national monument also contains Canyon del Muerto, or "canyon of the dead," named for the prehistoric burial remains discovered in a cave in the canyon by James Stevenson, who led an expedition in the area in 1882. The prehistoric sites tell of a more peaceful time in the canyon's history than does the written record of the area since the white man's arrival in the early 1800s.

The fiercely independent Navajo, who had uneasy relationships with the Europeans and many of their Native American neighbors, chose the intricate canyons of the Canyon de Chelly area as refuge against pursuers and intruders on many occasions. The entire area was fortress-like in its natural state.

In 1805, the Spanish, under the command of Lt. Colonel Antonio Narbona, engaged the Navajo in a day-long battle in Canyon del Muerto. Navajo men, women and children took shelter in a cave, now aptly called Massacre Cave, near the top of the Canyon. Narbona's troops fired down on the defenseless women and children from a vantage point on the canyon rim above. When the slaughter ended, more than 100 Navajos, including women and children, were dead and 33 were taken prisoner. The total cost to the Spaniards was a single soldier who lost his footing and fell to the canyon floor during the encounter.

Narbona, in his report to the governor in Santa Fe, had an entirely different account of the confrontation. He stated that 115 Navajo were killed, including 90 warriors, and 33 taken prisoner. No mention was made of the women or children. He later substantiated his claims with a package containing the ears of 84 Navajo, with an apology for the pairs that were missing. It is presumed these pairs were obviously too small to be mistaken for those of adults and were either not removed in the first place, or discarded in shame at a later date. The Navajo prisoners were enslaved by the Spaniards.

The Navajo had learned the effectiveness of arrows and stones against range of the white man's rifles and kept a relatively low profile throughout the remaining years of Spanish influence in the region. The Navajo, like the Apache, had always led an existence supplemented by raiding other tribes and they continued this practice against the Europeans invading their homelands. When the region passed from Spanish and Mexican control to

Left: Iron oxide patinas stain cliff walls above the cave sheltering White House Ruin. Anasazi structures in Canyon de Chelly and Canyon del Muerto were abandoned by AD 1300.
PHOTO BY DICK DIETRICH

Right: "Desert Varnish," long streaks of oxide laden chemicals, stains the walls of Canyon de Chelly. The streaks, although they appear wet, are dry to the touch.
PHOTO BY DICK DIETRICH

the Americans following signing of the Treaty of Guadalupe Hidalgo in 1848, the Navajo once again found themselves at odds with the white man.

Raiding by Navajos increased during the mid-1800s to levels that caused white settlers to seek retaliation. In 1863, the United States Army, under command of Brigadier General James Henry Carleton, sent Christopher "Kit" Carson, the former mountain man and Indian scout, into the field to engage the Navajo. Carson, commissioned a colonel of volunteers, was dispatched by the ruthless Carleton under the following orders: "All Indian men of that tribe are to be killed whenever and wherever you find them; the women and children will not be harmed, but you will take them prisoner." Carson's orders were crystal clear; he was not to make any attempt at peace, but was required eliminate all Navajo men.

In the summer of 1863, Carson gathered 736 volunteers consisting of Spanish settlers, Utes, Zuñis and even some Hopis– all who were unsympathetic to the Navajo– and set out to systematically complete his assigned task. On their route to Canyon de Chelly, Carson and his volunteers burned Navajo houses, killed their sheep and destroyed their fields. His attacks were so effective that by September large numbers of Navajo began to surrender. Many sought refuge at Fort Defiance, where they were given food and protection against Carson's marauding army.

Bands of Navajo fled in all directions– some joined with other tribes while others hid in remote northern areas. By January of 1864, the only Navajo still at large were in the area of Canyon de Chelly.

When Carson arrived at the entrance to the canyon that cold January he knew the battle was all but won. The Navajo had long used the canyon as a summer home, but were not equipped to survive the area in winter. Carson, to his credit, sent Carleton dispatches arguing there were too few Navajo left in the canyon to justify the hardships his troops would face in a winter campaign. The general, unfortunately for the remaining Navajo, felt a decisive victory would achieve lasting psychological effect on the Navajo everywhere and ordered Carson to proceed into the canyon.

By April of 1864, cold and hunger forced the final surrender of the Navajo in Canyon de Chelly and more than 8,000 began what became known as the "Long Walk" to their place of exile at Fort Sumner, New Mexico. Bosque Redondo, the Navajo's reservation, was a treeless, barren land where thousands of Navajo men, women and children died through exposure to the white man's diseases and from exposure to the elements. After four years, the army acknowledged their error in judgement and let the Navajo return to their traditional homelands in northern Arizona, the location of their present reservation.

The four years spent at Bosque Redondo were a sad and painful time for the Navajo. Fortunately, they are a bright and enterprising people and used their years of confinement to learn from other captives, and their captors, as much as they could about the changing world they found themselves thrust into. It was during the years at Bosque Redondo the Navajo learned the art of jewelry making for which they have since become famous.

KIT CARSON, INDIAN FIGHTER

It is the general nature of heroes and legends to grow tall in stature, gain incredible powers, and acquire a genteel manner as tales of their heroics are handed down through the ages. Christopher "Kit" Carson, the famous mountain man and Indian fighter, was no exception to this long-standing rule.

Born in Kentucky in 1809, Kit never learned to read or write. In fact, he never spent much time indoors. At age 15, he was apprenticed to a saddle maker in Missouri, but mending leather held little appeal for the young Carson and he soon ran away.

He traveled to Santa Fe, New Mexico, as a stock tender on a caravan, not as a famous hunter or Indian scout as the legends now have it. In 1826, Kit spent the winter in Taos with an old mountain man named Kincade, who taught the teenager the basics of frontier life over the winter.

The following two years were spent as a cook for Ewing Young, the famous mountain man, who was acting as a fur trapper and teamster for the Santa Rica Copper Mine. In August of 1829, Carson was finally signed on as a fur trapper on an expedition to California.

It was during this California expedition Carson first proved his ability at tracking and killing Indians. Near San Rafael, he tracked down a party of "mission Indians," tame Indians that had grown tired of toiling in servitude to the Franciscans and decided to leave the mission. Carson killed a large number of the escapees and forced the survivors to return to the mission. Kit enjoyed being an Indian fighter and tales of him singlehandedly taking on 50 or 60 Indians grew as he proudly stoked the fires of his own legend. Carson was undeniably eager to do battle with Indians and would rather engage them in combat than avoid confrontation.

In the early years of his career, he encountered a number of difficult situations on the frontier and in the wilderness. In 1834, he was treed by two enraged Grizzly Bears, an incident he later recalled in his memoirs as his "worst difficult." In the summer of 1835, at a trappers rendezvous in Wyoming, Carson killed a French-Canadian named Shunan in a hand-to-hand brawl. This murder was said to have taken place over the attentions of an Indian girl Carson later took as his wife.

In true mountain man fashion, Kit took two Indian wives. The first, an Arapaho girl named WaaNibe, died shortly after the birth of Kit's daughter Adaline from mountain fever. Around 1840, Carson took a Cheyenne girl named Making Out Road as his second wife. This union dissolved rather quickly as a result of her violent temper.

Above: Christopher "Kit" Carson, Indian fighter, scout and mountain man.
PHOTO COURTESY ARIZONA HISTORICAL SOCIETY

Kit Carson had a large impact in the settling of hostile Indian activities in Arizona. While the fictional Kit Carson was performing daring exploits in magazine articles and paperback books, the real Kit Carson was attempting to rescue a white woman being held by Apaches. During the winter of 1849, Carson and a troop of soldiers rode into the Dragoon Mountains to rescue the captive, Mrs. J. M. White. When they entered the Indian camp, Carson's companion and guide, Antoine Leroux, counseled a parley. During this delay the Apache killed Mrs. White and escaped. Upon searching the abandoned Apache camp, Kit came upon a copy of Charles Averill's *Kit Carson, Prince of the Goldhunters,* which portrayed a fictional account of Carson rescuing a maiden from renegade Indians.

Carson was dispatched, in 1863, by General James H. Carleton to bring the Navajo to their knees in the Canyon de Chelly region. Carleton's orders demanded no less than genocide of the Navajo males. Carson was decidedly the man for the job. He killed the Navajo, their sheep and cattle, and destroyed their crops. Navajo lucky enough to escape fled in all directions, some ironically finding protection from Carson and his band of marauders with the U.S. Army at Fort Defiance. The survivors of this brutal campaign were forced-marched to the Bosque Redondo Reservation, where thousands died.

Right: Spider Rock, Canyon de Chelly. According to Navajo legends, there were two beings in the beginning of time: Spider Woman, the goddess of earth; and Tawa, the goddess of the skies. Navajo children were taught that if they did not behave, Spider Woman would take them to the top of Spider Rock and throw them off.
PHOTO BY JERRY JACKA

Following pages: Betatakin, a Navajo name that translates as "ledge house," is protected in an alcove that measures 452 feet in height, by 370 feet in width, and is 135 feet in depth.
PHOTO BY MICHAEL FATALI

MONUMENT VALLEY

Monument Valley Navajo Tribal Park is sometimes referred to as the "Eighth Wonder of the World," a reference to the haunting beauty of its massive buttes, towering sandstone pinnacles and windswept sands. Monument Valley is a true geological valley; bordered on the east and south by Comb Reef, the west by Hoskinini Mesa and the north by the San Juan River. This area is known throughout the world for its sunrises and sunsets and for the geological formations found within its 40-by-50 mile boundaries.

Although Monument Valley is so barren that only a few Navajo shepherds can find subsistence working the land today, it was once home to several hundred Anasazi. Water was always scarce in this arid region and the earlier inhabitants are thought to have constructed small dams to trap and hold flash flood runoff that coursed down arroyos after the rains. Anasazi in Monument Valley farmed small plots along arroyo edges, releasing the runoff to irrigate crops of corn, beans, pumpkins and squash. This meager existence did not attract hostile raiders and lack of water discouraged any travel through the area. The Anasazi to enjoyed a peaceful existence in Monument Valley for several centuries.

Several hundred Anasazi dwellings can still be found within the boundaries of Monument Valley, most of them are small and many are neither marked nor named. Favored sites were in isolated canyons. Some were constructed unobtrusively in the walls of the cliffs.

In the later part of the 13th century, a severe drought occurred in the region and the Anasazi left their Monument Valley homes to join clans in areas with greater access to water. Today, all that remains of the Anasazi occupation of the valley are abandoned dwellings, pottery fragments and projectile points.

The departure of the Anasazi left the area open for settlement by the Navajo, who are still in residence today. The Navajo live in tune with nature, leading simple lives herding sheep, making their traditional rugs and creating jewelry. Their entire existence is geared to the preservation of local water supplies. They never build their hogans (mud and timber dwellings) near a water hole. They believe all things were created by one God and keep well away from water sources so that insects, birds and animals have equal access and a chance for survival.

The remoteness of Monument Valley, along with spectacular scenery and a unique geology, have attracted a variety of visitors over the years. Outlaws on the lam have fled to the area; Kit Carson tried unsuccessfully to round up Monument Valley Navajo during his ruthless campaign to eradicate the Navajo; Silver and Uranium prospectors combed the area in search of mineral wealth; and tourists from around the world visited to view the natural wonder of the valley. Many films were made on location in Monument Valley, most during the 1930s, including John Wayne's *Stagecoach*. Through the years, the Navajo continue to tend to their own ways as best they can.

Left: Totem Pole and Yei Bichei spires show the ravages of erosion over time in the vast expanse of Monument Valley. Windswept sands resemble plowed fields of a more fertile land.
PHOTO BY JERRY JACKA

Right: The Mittens, two of the most distinctive buttes in Monument Valley, during one of the spectacular sunsets the area is famous for.
PHOTO BY JERRY JACKA

Navajo National Monument

A principal home for the Kayenta Anasazi, Navajo National Monument contains three of the best preserved and most elaborate cliff dwellings known: Keet Seel, Betatakin and Inscription House.

Kayenta Anasazi were the premier potters among the Anasazi and produced the most advanced multi-colored pottery of their time. Until approximately AD 1250, they lived in villages in open areas. Abruptly, they began to construct elaborate cliff dwelling in remote canyons far from their fields and abandoned life in the open villages. This may have been the result of threats by other Native American groups entering the region at the time.

Betatakin and Keet Seel were built into the cliffs of Tsegi Canyon. Betatakin, a Navajo name meaning "ledge house," has 135 rooms that are sheltered in an alcove measuring 452 feet high, 370 feet wide and 135 feet deep. Keet Seel, which translates from the Navajo as "broken pottery," has more than 150 rooms and six kivas. Keet Seel's name reflects the large quantity of pottery shards in evidence at the site. Inscription House, in nearby Nitsin Canyon, is a three story structure that contained about 80 rooms and one kiva.

Kayenta Anasazi abandoned their canyon homes around AD 1300, and are thought to have moved to the Hopi mesas. There is some evidence of decreased rainfall throughout the region during this period and there is some speculation they moved to find more arable land. Whatever their reasons, they must have been quite compelling to cause the complete abandonment of these elaborate structures.

Below: Keet Seel, discovered in 1895 by Al and Richard Wetherill, is one of the largest and best preserved ruins found in the Southwest, with more than 150 rooms and six kivas.
PHOTO BY CHARLES CHANLEY

Right: Window Rock, a natural arch 50 feet wide located a few miles south of Fort Defiance, is near the center of Navajo tribal administration in the village of Window Rock.
PHOTO BY JERRY JACKA

Following pages: Monument Valley's haunting beauty, towering buttes and natural spires have long been prized by film makers. John Ford filmed the movie *Stagecoach* here in 1938.
PHOTO BY JERRY SIEVE

THE HOPI

The Hopi, abbreviated from Hopituh Shi-nu-mu, which means "the peaceful people," are the only remaining pueblo dwellers in Arizona. The Hopi have occupied their domain for hundreds of years in villages on top of high, barren mesas in northern Arizona.

In 1878, Thomas V. Keam, an Englishman, started a trading post near the three Hopi mesas in an area that came to be known as Keams Canyon. Keams named the mesas "First Mesa," "Second Mesa" and "Third Mesa" in the opposite order that the Hopi referred to their ancestral sites. In ancient times, these mesas, the three southern prongs of Black Mesa, provided the Hopi with natural protection from their traditional enemies.

In 1543, Spaniards, under the command of Don Pedro de Tovar, first visited the Hopi. They brought gifts and established a camp near Kawaiokuh, which today is a ruin. From the Hopi, the Spaniards learned of the Colorado River and the Grand Canyon.

Don Pedro de Tovar ordered Captain Garcia de Cardenas north to search for the Canyon

Above: Hopi pottery from Northern Arizona.
COURTESY KEAMS CANYON ARTS AND CRAFTS
PHOTO BY JERRY JACKA

and the river. The Spanish were unimpressed by the region and its lack of precious minerals and they did not return to visit the Hopi again for the following forty years.

When the Spanish returned, they attempted to convert the Hopi to Christianity, which they continued to do until the Hopi joined the other pueblos in the Pueblo Revolt of 1680.

Spanish intervention meant little to the Hopi; they were not interested in the white man's God, and their remote and arid region did little to attract white settlers.

Old Oraibi vies with the village of Acoma, in New Mexico, for the distinction of being the oldest continuously occupied village in North America. Both were established around 1100 AD. Old Oraibi was one of the largest Hopi towns until 1906, when arguments over the education of Hopi children brought about the founding of Hotevilla, Bacabi, and New Oraibi on Third Mesa.

The Hopi have always been concerned with the preservation of their lands. For centuries they have been completely surrounded by the Navajo, who had been their traditional enemy. Through a series of treaties between the Navajo and Hopi, the federal government has attempted unsuccessfully to resolve their territorial conflicts on numerous occasions. Disputes over the ownership of these lands continue in Washington to this day.

The Hopi social organization is based upon a clan system, with strong ties to the mother. Homes are built adjacent to the mother's home, and men join their wife's clan upon marriage. Women own their houses, food, seeds for planting, springs, wells and their gardens. Men do the hunting, farming, herding and yarn and leather work. An important aspect of the social structure is curing, which is under the control of medicine societies known as kachina. All Hopi are members of one of the numerous kachina cults.

The Hopi conduct many of their ceremonies to ensure the proper passage of the seasons, promote fertility in plants and animals, to encourage rain, and ensure hunting success. Many of these elaborate presentations are open to visitors.

Snake Dances are among the best known and most involved. Men and boys of the Snake and Antelope fraternities emerge from their kivas, painted and costumed, and search the surrounding countryside for four days gathering snakes. On the day of the Snake Dance, the Antelope priests line up in the plaza and await arrival of the Snake priests.

THE KACHINA

The kachina, or katsina, are believed by the pueblo peoples to be supernatural beings who dwell in mountains, lakes, and springs and bestow many blessings on the pueblo people. Kachina are the spirits of all things, from the birds in the sky to the corn in the fields. Among the Zuñi people they are known as koko.

Most kachina are benevolent in nature and are responsible for rain, successful crops, and good health. Others are ogres, or demons, and are used to represent disciplinary functions. It is said that ogres will eat children who do not obey the kachinas, or do not behave themselves.

Kachinas, according to pueblo legends, were real beings and would visit the pueblo people when they were sad, or lonely, and would dance for them. The kachina brought gifts and taught arts and crafts, how to build villages, cultivate crops, and how to hunt. As time went by, the pueblo people began to take the kachina for granted and lost respect for their benevolence. Violent struggles broke out between the pueblos and the supernatural beings. Finally, the kachina quit visiting the pueblos.

Because the kachina truly cared for the pueblo people, they taught some of the faithful their ceremonies, how to make the kachina masks and costumes, and permitted them, as long as they were pure of heart, to act as if they were kachinas. If the kachina ceremony was enacted properly, real kachinas would appear and take possession of the masked dancers.

Although all members of the tribe are initiated into kachina societies, only men are allowed to impersonate the kachinas.

Kachinas are represented in various ways, all connected in the minds of the pueblo people. First, they are considered human, although they

Above: Kachina sculpted of wood by Hopi Dennis Tewa. Kachina play an important role in the ceremonies of pueblo people and are revered by the Hopi of all ages.
PHOTO BY JERRY JACKA

are not; they are also the masked, costumed and painted dancers who appear as impersonators of the spiritual kachinas to perform rites and ceremonies; and they are also wooden figurines, small carved images of the life-sized beings, revered by the pueblo people.

Pueblo children use the carved figurines to study the kachina's ways and to learn many of life's lessons. Adults collect them in much the same manner Christians collect religious images.

Below: Hopi wicker plaque by Dora Tawahongva; small coiled bowl by Gertina Lomakema and a large coiled bowl with butterfly and corn designs by Martha Kooyestewa.
COURTESY KEAMS CANYON ARTS AND CRAFTS
PHOTO BY JERRY JACKA

Upon arrival of the Snake priests, gourds are rattled to emulate sounds of rattlesnakes, and priests begin a deep sonorous chorus. As the chorus reaches a climax, the Snake men form groups of three and reach into a cottonwood bough, where a priest, who is hidden inside, hands them a snake. The snake is placed in the mouth of the Snake man, while his two assistants trail behind to control the snake. As many as 70 or 80 snakes may be involved in the ceremony.

As the ceremony continues, Hopi women sprinkle corn meal on the snakes and dancers. When all of the snakes are freed and placed within a circle, they dart in all directions. Pandemonium ensues among Hopi and visitors alike, until all of the snakes have been collected. The Snake men rush out of the village and down trails to free the snakes. As the

Above: Hopi overlay jewelry is produced by soldering two pieces of silver together. The top piece contains a finely cut design element of highly polished silver designed to contrast with the piece below.   PHOTO BY JERRY JACKA

ceremony ends the villagers relax and a four day festival begins.

The Hopi are accomplished artisans and craftsmen well known for the high quality of their kachina carvings, watercolor paintings, basketry, pottery and jewelry making.

Early Hopi silverwork designs were inspired by Zuñi and Navajo silversmiths during the end of the 19th century. Today, their inlay jewelry technique is especially popular as is their work with turquoise and coral.

During the early 1900s, silver was difficult for the Hopi to acquire. Sometimes when Hopi men ran out of the precious metal they rode or walked to Winslow and "acquired" the silverware of local restaurants. They then took the silverware to the nearest railroad track and waited for a train to compress the metal into a pliable material.

THE ART OF THE NAVAJO

The Navajo, Athabascans who migrated into the Southwest from Canada more than 1000 years ago, were nomadic hunter-gathers. Always intelligent and creative people, they were quick to learn the arts and crafts of the more sedentary pueblos they encountered.

From the pueblos the Navajo learned the art of weaving, at first weaving blankets for trade items and later switching to rugs as machine woven blankets, softer and much cheaper to create, replaced the demand for woven blankets.

Early Navajo weavings were primarily of cotton and natural fibers. Weaving in wool did not begin until about AD 1600, after sheep were introduced to the Southwest by the Spanish. Due to the fragile nature of the earlier fibers, few examples of this work remains. The earliest known examples were discovered along with burial remains in Massacre Cave in Canyon del Muerto.

Navajo jewelry making is synonymous with silver and turquoise. Many believe turquoise has benign powers that ward off calamities and

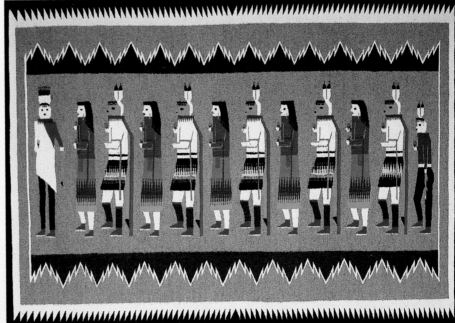

many of life's hazards. Although this theory has yet to have been give a basis in scientific fact, the stones make beautiful good luck charms.

Although metal work by the Navajo dates to the middle of the 19th century, all early work was in iron or copper. While the Navajo were detained at Fort Sumner following the Long Walk, Navajo men learned the craft of metal working. No silver work was fashioned until the Navajo left Bosque Redondo and returned to their homelands.

Early production methods were crude, but the quality of Navajo work gradually increased until today's high standards were achieved. Before the 1880s, no settings were made. Around this period bits of glass, beads and garnets were incorporated into Navajo designs. After 1900, turquoise began to appear in increasing quantities.

A variety of silver articles are currently being produced by the Navajo; conchas for belts, rings, buttons, earrings, bracelets, necklaces, hat bands and more. The most common necklace designs are made of large, hollow silver beads that are separated by flower-shaped pendants. These are commonly called "squash blossom" necklaces because of the pendant features but were in fact modeled after pomegranate blossoms the Navajo observed in earlier Spanish work.

Left: Finely crafted silver and turquoise jewelry by Navajo jeweler Thomas Singer.
PHOTO BY JERRY JACKA

Above: Navajo Yei-Bi-Chai rug by Lucy Nakai.
PHOTO BY JERRY JACKA

ANCIENT INHABITANTS

Cliff dwellings allowed early Native Americans an opportunity to enjoy a modicum of security in an often hostile environment. Access was normally up steep trails that were easily defended by a few people. If intruders found their way up to the dwellings, removable ladders kept them from gaining entrance through customary second floor openings.

The first residents of Arizona arrived from Asia, crossing the Bering Strait on an ancient land bridge exposed during the last Ice Age, at least 13,000 years ago and perhaps thousands of years earlier. These early inhabitants are called the Elephant Hunters.

The Elephant Hunters were nomads who found Arizona far more tropical than it is today. Their existence depended on hunting large prehistoric beasts; mammoths, elephants, mastodons, camels, bison and horses. They used teamwork to kill prey with stone spearheads that utilized detachable foreshafts. When the main shaft was worked free by a wounded animal, the smaller foreshaft would remain embedded and continue to let blood.

Two kill sites were discovered in Arizona, dating approximately 11,000 years ago, and excavated by University of Arizona archaeologists during the 1950s. At the first site, along the banks of Greenbush Creek near Naco, an extinct mammoth was excavated. Eight stone spearheads were found within the body of an animal that had been thirteen feet tall. At the second site, along the San Pedro River on the Lehner Ranch, bones of nine elephants were unearthed along with those of a primitive horse (a species that was extinct long before the arrival of the Europeans), a bison and a tapir. The ashes from two fires found in the vicinity, probably made to roast the meat, were carbon dated to about 11,000 years ago.

As the polar ice cap melted, Arizona's climate became increasingly drier. The vegetation the large mammals foraged upon became sparse and these species were replaced by smaller animals. Descendants of the Elephant Hunters, the Cochise people, adjusted to an environment with fewer resources.

The Cochise people, so named because many of their remains have been found along creek banks in Cochise County, hunted small animals and gathered nuts, berries, roots and grains to supplement their diets. Around 4,000 years ago, Arizona Native Americans learned to cultivate crops from trading partners from the south and began to adopt a less nomadic existence as they remained in an area to grow and await harvesting of their crops.

Arizona was home to all three major prehistoric cultures found in the Southwest; the Hohokam, the Mogollon and the Anasazi. The Hohokam lived in river valleys of the southern desert and were an agricultural group. The Mogollon were the descendants of the Cochise and were primarily hunters and gatherers. The Anasazi were cliff dwellers in northern areas of the state. Other prehistoric cultures include the Patayan, who lived along the banks of the Colorado River; the Sinagua who lived in the Verde Valley and near the San Francisco Peaks in northern Arizona; and the Salado, who were of Anasazi origin and lived in the Tonto Basin in east-central Arizona.

The Hohokam built a civilization that lasted for around 1,700 years. They were the first

Left: Montezuma Castle, a Late Stage dwelling of the Sinagua culture, was constructed during the 13th century. The structure was erroneously named after the famous chief.
PHOTO BY BOB CLEMENZ

Right: Native American artists painted or carved their drawings on rock surfaces, each drawing thought to symbolize an important event. The carvings are *petroglyphs*, made by scratching designs into the rock surface. The paintings are *pictographs,* created by painting the surface.
PHOTO BY STEVE BRUNO

southwestern farmers to exhibit a knowledge of irrigation. The Hohokam dug a series of gravity-fed canals along the Salt and Gila rivers, some as much as 30-40 feet wide and up to 15 feet deep. More than 200 miles of canals have been traced in the Salt River Valley alone that are credited to the Hohokam.

Irrigation enabled the Hohokam to establish more permanent villages and towns, which in turn led to a higher quality of living.

During the 15th century, the Hohokam left their villages for reasons that are still debated. Their farmlands may have become unarable, a condition caused by floods or a raising of

the water table due to continued saturation. The name Hohokam is a Pima word meaning "those who have vanished." It is currently thought the Hohokam were the ancestors of the Pima and Papago (Tohono O'odham).

The Mogollon lived in the mountains in small villages, normally less than twenty dwelling units, built into a mountain or hill. Using pithouse construction techniques, the dwellings were partially underground and were usually entered down a ramp on the east

Left: Mogollon Rim bathed in evening light.
PHOTO BY BOB CLEMENZ

Above: Tuzigoot, a Sinagua pueblo, had seventy-seven ground floor rooms.   PHOTO BY BOB CLEMENZ

Below: Winter sunset.   PHOTO BY STEVE BRUNO

side. A large kiva was the central part of the village, a place of communal gathering.

Ancestors of the Mogollon were the first Southwestern culture to grow corn, which they received from trading parties from what is now Mexico. The Mogollon were also the first to make pottery. Prior to the introduction of pottery, foods were cooked in baskets by placing heated stones and food together in the basket. This process was limited and very hard on the baskets. Water was stored in baskets lined with pitch.

During the early 1300s, the Mogollon began to disappear. It is thought several groups were completely absorbed by the Anasazi and that others were ancestors of today's Hopi and Zuñi, a theory supported by both groups who claim the Mogollon as ancestors. It is also possible some groups migrated south to Mexico and became the Tarahumara Indians. It is probable one, or both, of these theories may be correct.

The Sinagua were farmers who inhabited the area around the San Francisco Peaks beginning around AD 500. Sinagua is derived from a Spanish phrase sin "without" and agua

"water." An apt description since they relied solely on rainfall to water their crops.

The Sinagua lived peaceful existences in their timber pithouses until, in AD 1064, the Sunset Crater volcano erupted and streams of lava flowed onto Sinagua lands. When the volcano finished erupting, in early 1065, more than 800 square miles were covered with volcanic ash and the resulting crater was 400 feet deep.

Above: Wupatki had more than 100 rooms, a large amphitheater and a stone Hohokam-style ball court.   PHOTO BY MICHAEL FATALI

With the eruption of the volcano, the Sinagua fled from their homes. When they returned to the area several years later, the soil had been greatly enriched by the volcanic ash. This new fertility attracted other groups including the Anasazi, Mogollon and Hohokam.

These more advanced groups had a great influence on the Sinagua, who absorbed their customs and skills. From the Anasazi they learned to build pueblos; irrigation and canals were a direct influence of the Hohokam; and from the Mogollon they learned the art of

pottery making. With the new skills they acquired they built the multi-roomed pueblos at Wupatki, Tuzigoot and Montezuma Castle.

Montezuma Castle National Monument has two distinct locations: Montezuma Castle, two five-story pueblos built into the cliffs above Beaver Creek in Verde Valley; and Montezuma Well, a limestone sink partially filled from an underground spring that flows at 1.5 million gallons per day.

The Sinagua abandoned Verde Valley around AD 1425. This may have been the result of a prolonged drought, warfare or disease.

THE ANASAZI

The Anasazi (Hisatsinom) first appeared in Arizona around 2,000 years ago. They are thought descendants of the archaic Desert Culture that inhabited the Southwest from about 6000 BC, or a branch of Mogollon who wandered into the region from the south.

They are best known for the cliff dwellings they inhabited in the later years of their civilization. The ruins at Navajo National Monument and Canyon de Chelly National Monument are among the best preserved ruins found in North America and have attracted attention from around the world since their discovery during the late 1800s.

For the first 1,000 years of their civilization the Anasazi lived in open-country communities. Their earlier pithouse dwellings were built three to five feet in the ground with roofs supported by poles and beams covered with brush and mud.

Early Anasazi lived in small villages near fields where they grew corn, squash and beans. They gathered wild foods including agave, walnuts, pinyon nuts, acorns, yucca, prickly pear, Indian ricegrass and wild potatoes; gathered other plants for use as medicines, fuel and building materials; and hunted game including elk, deer, pronghorn, mountain sheep, rabbit, turkey, birds, fish and rodents. Archeologists believe, based on this pattern of living in open country without the protection afforded by later cliff dwellings, the Anasazi had relatively few, or perhaps no, natural enemies during these early years.

The various periods of the Anasazi culture have been defined by scientists as Basketmaker I, Basketmaker II, Basketmaker III, Pueblo I, Pueblo II, Pueblo III, Pueblo IV and Pueblo V. The earliest

The Colorado River flows by an Anasazi ruin in the Grand Canyon.   PHOTO BY TOM TILL

Anasazi were the Basketmaker II who lived from about AD 1 to about AD 500. (The Basketmaker I designation is used for earlier archaic cultures believed by many to have been ancestors of the Anasazi.) Basketmaker II people grew crops of corn and squash, hunted with spears and spear throwers called atlatls, and gathered wild foods they stored in baskets. They lived in caves, rock shelters and, in some areas, built circular log houses with slightly depressed floors.

The Basketmaker III period, from around AD 500 to AD 700, brought a period of major change to the Anasazi. Pottery was developed which proved more practical for storing water and cooking hot foods; beans, which provided a good source of protein, were added to Anasazi crops; the bow and arrow replaced the spear and atlatl; and pithouse construction began. This all added

stability to Anasazi life, although gathering wild plants remained important. Pottery allowed better storage of surplus food and the Anasazi became less vulnerable to climactic cycles.

The Pueblo I stage began around AD 700 and lasted until AD 900. During this period, pithouses were beginning to be replaced by above ground dwellings. Painted pottery emerged; with black-on-white, red-on-orange and black-on-red types appearing; and there is evidence agriculture increased in importance and sophistication.

During Pueblo II, from AD 900 to 1100, kivas (communal rooms for special purposes) began appearing. During this stage, the population significantly increased as numerous small villages appeared over a wide range.

Pueblo III, from AD 1100 to 1300, found larger masonry villages, some several stories tall, in caves and on mesa tops that were easy to defend, suggesting a new threat from outside forces. Crafts were refined and trade with the neighboring cultures intensified. At the end of Pueblo III, for reasons still not completely understood, Arizona Anasazi sites were largely abandoned.

The Pueblo IV stage, from AD 1300 until the arrival of the Spanish in 1598, found the Anasazi in the northern areas moving south to join the Hopi and Zuñi. Eastern Anasazi pueblos continued to grow into larger settlements that often housed hundreds, or thousands, of people.

The Anasazi are debated among many who glamorize their departure from ancestral homes with wild tales with mysterious overtones. The pueblo peoples of Arizona and New Mexico have always recognized the Anasazi as their ancestors.

THE PETRIFIED FOREST

Coelophysis, a vicious predator, inhabited the area that is now the Petrified Forest during the late Triassic Period (225 million years ago). Although small by standards of dinosaurs that followed, they grew to about eight feet in length.

Discovered several thousand years ago by the Anasazi, the Petrified Forest has hundreds of prehistoric ruins, and other sites, ranging in size from one-room shelters to Puerco Pueblo, which contained more than 100 rooms. Agate House, a partially reconstructed pueblo, was built using petrified wood.

The petrified logs were a mystery to Native American groups in the vicinity of the Petrified Forest. Major John Wesley Powell, during one of his Colorado Plateau expeditions, noted that the Paiutes believed the petrified logs were arrow shafts of *Shinuav*, the thunder god, and that local Navajos were convinced the logs were bones of the monster *Yiesto*, "the great giant," killed by their ancestors when they arrived in the Southwest. Native Americans made use of the petrified wood, carving tools from the stone and using it as a building material. It is not known if they ever realized the material they carved had once been wood.

Today, we know the Petrified Forest was formed by *fossilization*, a process that is still not completely understood. Normally, when a living organism dies its remains are either eaten by scavengers or decay sets in and the remaining organism is broken down by the elements, insects and bacteria. In the Petrified Forest, these processes did not always occur and remains of some organisms were fossilized. Moisture, supply of oxygen, temperature, burial depth, elements in the surrounding sediments and other factors may contribute to the overall effect on a potential fossil.

Most of the wood and bone found in the Petrified Forest have been petrified, or turned to stone. Although several different kinds of petrification took place within the Petrified Forest, there are two common types present in the the area.

The first type, which includes a majority of samples within the park, occurs when all the organic matter in the potential fossil is replaced by mineral matter, resulting in a fossil that has the external form of the object, but little or none of its internal structure remains.

The second kind of petrification is called *permineralization*. In this process, the cellular details of the fossil can still be observed with a microscope and only a portion of the object becomes petrified, while much of the remaining organic matter is unchanged.

The Petrified Forest contains an incredible quantity of fossils, petrified or preserved by compression, detailing the flora and fauna of the ancient forests of the late Triassic Period (225 million years ago). Fossils of ancient fish, including two species of sharks, have been discovered along with remains of numerous reptiles and dinosaurs, including *phytosaurs*, large crocodile-like reptiles that measured as much as thirty feet long.

During the late 1890s, visitation increased to levels threatening remaining examples of petrified wood and fossils. Convinced the area was in danger of over exploitation, President Theodore Roosevelt established Petrified Forest National Monument in 1906.

Left: Logs in Crystal Forest display a rainbow of color. The wood has been totally replaced by quartz containing traces of other substances, creating the variety of colors.
PHOTO BY JERRY SIEVE

Right: These logs on the edge of Blue Mesa were petrified during the Triassic Period of the Mesozoic Era, around 225 million years ago.
PHOTO BY DICK DIETRICH

THE MOUNTAIN REGION

Although all regions of Arizona contain some mountainous terrain, the area referred to as the Mountain Region refers to the central mountain belt that crosses the state diagonally from the northwest to the southeast. This region includes the arid mountains in the Kingman area and increases in width, rainfall and elevation through the central part of the state reaching an elevation of 12,670 feet at Mount Humphreys, one of the San Francisco Peaks in the Flagstaff area, and continues southeast to Mexico. The southern area of the mountain region includes Mount Graham, at an elevation of 10,720 feet in the Pinaleno Range, and Mount Lemon, at 9,150 feet, in the Santa Catalinas north of Tucson.

Most Arizona mountain ranges are between 25 and 75 miles long and 5 to 15 miles wide, with peaks rising to elevations between 4,000 and 6,000 feet, and are drained by tributaries of the Gila and Salt rivers. These rivers cut deep channels through the mountains in the eastern and central areas of the state before they join the Colorado River just above the Gulf of Mexico. In recent years, much of their water has been stored in man-made lakes behind dams on the Gila, Verde and Salt rivers.

The Mountain Region played an important role in the history and development of Arizona. Gold, silver and copper deposits lured early settlers in search of mineral wealth. Many towns in mountain areas owe their beginnings to early prospectors including Bisbee, Tombstone, Morenci, Globe and Jerome. The most productive grazing lands are found in the mountain regions, where grass-covered highlands began attracting ranchers in the early 1870s.

The early white settlers in mountain regions of Arizona were fur trappers, better known as "mountain men," searching for valuable skins, primarily Beaver pelts. Their activities led to the exploration of the Gila, Salt, Verde, San Pedro, San Francisco, Colorado and other Arizona rivers. Famous mountain men in the region included: Kit Carson, Pauline Weaver, James Ohio Pattie, "Old Bill" Williams, Jedediah Smith, Ewing Young, "Pegleg" Smith, Milton Sublette, Miguel Rubidoux and Antoine Leroux.

Pauline Weaver made his fame as a master trapper, guide and prospector. James Ohio Pattie visited the region as early as 1826 and wrote about it in his famous book *Personal Narrative*. Jedediah Smith visited the Mojave Range on at least two occasions. Although no other "mountain man" was as famous as the legendary Kit Carson, it has long been difficult to separate fact from Carson's own tall tales regarding his life.

In 1863, Governor James Goodwin, the first territorial governor, chose a site in the pines along Granite Creek to become the Arizona Territory's first capital. Territorial Secretary Richard McCormick named the area Prescott, after historian William H. Prescott. The first capitol building housed the governor, territorial secretary and the legislature in a Ponderosa Pine log building. In 1867, the territorial capital moved to Tucson where it remained until 1877.

Arizona's mountains are home to the world's largest contiguous stand of Ponderosa Pine, *Pinus ponderosa,* also known as Yellow Pine. Much of the timber harvested by lumber mills in northern and eastern Arizona is Ponderosa Pine.

Left: Rainwater fills a hollowed Quaking Aspen, *Populus tremuloides,* in the White Mountains of eastern Arizona.
PHOTO BY JERRY JACKA

Right: Granite outcroppings rise dramatically from deep blue waters at Granite Dells.
PHOTO BY BOB CLEMENZ

Following pages: A view of the San Francisco Peaks from Locketts Meadow in early fall.
PHOTO BY MICHAEL FATALI

SEDONA

Sedona, located around one hundred miles north of Phoenix in central Arizona, has three attractions within its five hundred square mile region: Sedona, Oak Creek Canyon, and Red Rock Country. The area– from the southern boundaries of Red Rock Country, known for its portrayal in numerous western movies– to the 7,000 foot elevations at the top of Oak Creek Canyon near Flagstaff, is one of the state's most popular destinations.

The region contains a variety of physical environments that include elements of seven major biotic communities. These environments, from the Desert Grassland and Pinyon-Juniper Woodland to the Ponderosa Pine Forest, coupled with an extensive Riparian Community along the banks of Oak Creek, provide habitat for an impressive array of flora and fauna.

Much of Sedona's visual appeal is attributed to the geology of the region. Comprised of seven layers of sedimentary rock, the landscape offers some of the most spectacular rock formations in the world. The beauty of the area's buttes, pinnacles and monoliths have inspired man since they were first gazed upon. By examining the Redwall Limestone deposits, the oldest visible in the region, we can date the area to the Mississippian Period of the Paleozoic Era (330 million years ago), when the entire region was covered by the sea.

For 130 million years the seas advanced and retreated through the region, each time leaving a different sedimentary layer. These layers, and the fossils they contain, are still visible in the canyon walls. During the Triassic Period of the Mesozoic Era (200 million years ago), the ancient ocean retreated for a final time. Tidal flats, running streams and forces of wind and water erosion began to shape the remaining sedimentary deposits.

The arrival of man in the region has been dated to approximately 7,500 years ago. These early Native Americans were hunter-gatherers who have been identified, and dated, by the discovery of their projectile points and stone tools. Over the following 6,000 years, these primitive people slowly evolved into farmers and basket makers.

Around AD 700, the Archaics were absorbed, or replaced, by the Hakataya, who practiced dry farming and made pottery. During this same period, the Hohokam migrated into the region from the south and introduced irrigation. As the Hohokam prospered, the Hakataya moved into their villages.

In about AD 1200, the Sinagua migrated to the region and gradually assumed control, and merged with, the Hakataya and Hohokam. This new group is referred to as the Southern Sinagua by anthropologists. By the mid-1400s, the Southern Sinagua abandoned the region for reasons that are not fully understood. Within the next 200 years, the Yavapai and Tonto Apache arrived. They remain present in the region today.

Spanish explorer Antonio de Espejo entered the region, in 1583, on a mission searching for two missing Spanish Friars and in search of

Oak Creek Canyon features seven biotic communities– from Desert Grassland to Ponderosa Pine Forest. The area was named for the several species of oak trees, including Gray, Emory, Gambel's, Palmer, Wavy Leaf, Arizona White and Shrub Live oaks, found in the canyon.

Left: A palette of fall colors cloaks trees lining the banks of Oak Creek.
PHOTO BY BOB CLEMENZ

Right: Coffee Pot Rock, one of the more famous formations in Red Rock Country, shows the effects of 330 million years of geologic forces at work on sedimentary deposits in the region.
PHOTO BY JERRY JACKA

SEDONA CONTINUED...

mines south of the Hopi mesas. They were successful only in locating copper mines, not the more valuable gold and silver they sought. In 1598, another mineral-seeking expedition, this one under the command of Marcos Farfan de los Godos, entered the area and briefly encountered the Yavapai and Tonto Apache.

In the early 1800s, the American pioneers, trappers and prospectors, began to enter the region. Relations between settlers and area Native Americans remained amicable until the 1850s. By then, Yavapai-Apache subsistence patterns of hunting and gathering were being encroached upon by settlers and the Indians began to retaliate, stealing crops and, by 1860, open raiding was occurring.

Gen. George Crook arrived in the area, in 1872, and quickly ended hostilities.

By the end of 1865, the problem escalated to a point requiring the army to send troops, under command of Lt. Antonio Abeyita, from Fort Whipple in Prescott. Camp Lincoln, named after the president, was established. Three years later, to avoid confusion from a rash of facilities named after President Lincoln, the name was changed to Camp Verde. Although Camp Verde troops held their own in skirmishes with the Yavapai-Apache, many died during a malaria epidemic. In 1871, Camp Verde Indian Reservation was established for the Native

Americans living in the Verde Valley area. Many were less than content with reservation life, notably the Delshay and the Chalipun, and, with most of the Yavapai-Apache, left the reservation to continue raiding.

As raiding escalated, General George Crook was dispatched from Tucson to resolve the problem. His main tactic was to keep the hostiles on the move, wear them out and exhaust their food supplies. By April of 1873, Crook's campaign was successful and the hostile groups had surrendered to the U.S. Army.

Gen. Crook tried convincing Native Americans that life on the reservation could not only be tolerated, it could also be profitable by growing surplus crops for sale to the military and local settlers. Unfortunately, overly ambitious ranchers and uncaring government officials succeeded in having the reservation abolished and the lands promised to the Yavapai-Apache were once again absorbed by white settlers. During winter of 1875, some 1400 Yavapai-Tonto Apache were forced marched to the San Carlos Indian Reservation in east-central Arizona, resulting

Above: C.J. "Bear" Howard, an escaped convict from California, with a gallery of admirers, his hunting dogs and the bodies of two Black Bears killed in Oak Creek Canyon.

in the deaths of nearly 100 people. They were not allowed to return to their homelands until the late 1890s.

The first permanent white settler in Sedona was John James "Jim" Thompson, who built a cabin in Oak Creek Canyon in 1876. During that same year, Beaver Head Stage Station was established twelve miles south of the present town of Sedona.

Sedona Schnebly migrated to the area in 1901.

Around 1880, C.J. "Bear" Howard, an escaped convict from California, built a cabin at the west fork of Oak Creek. Howard hunted bear in the area and sold the meat in Flagstaff. Over the years, Howard's cabin was expanded, becoming Mayhew's Lodge, and was visited by presidents, movie stars and celebrities from around the world.

In 1901, Theodore Schnebly and his wife, a Pennsylvania Dutch woman named Sedona, acquired 80 acres of land in the area. In 1902, Theodore applied for the first post office, which he hoped to name "Schnebly Station." His request was granted, but his name was rejected as too long. He submitted his wife's name and the area as since been called Sedona.

Below: A rainbow frames Pinyon Pine, One-seed Juniper and massive buttes near Dry Creek Road.
PHOTO BY JERRY JACKA

Right: Slide Rock in Oak Creek Canyon, a natural water slide created by erosion of the creek bed.
PHOTO BY SUZANNE CLEMENZ

Right: Bell Rock towers 550 feet above the Pinyon-Juniper Woodland. The flowering plants in the foreground are Agave, *Agave havardi,* also called century plants. As soon as the stalk starts to bloom the plant begins to die.
PHOTO BY MICHAEL FATALI

Left: Sunlight bathes the intimate confines of Oak Creek Canyon in the early fall.
PHOTO BY BOB CLEMENZ

Right: The Chapel of the Holy Cross, inspired by a Frank Lloyd Wright design executed by the architectural firm of Anshen and Allen, blends gracefully with surrounding formations.
PHOTO BY MICHAEL FATALI

Following pages: Cathedral Rock, a turreted sandstone butte, stands nearly 1,000 feet above Oak Creek at Red Rock Crossing.
PHOTO BY STEVE BRUNO

TAMING THE COLORADO RIVER...

Throughout this text we have discussed the forces of nature in the continuing erosion of the lands bordering the Colorado River. The river worked its changes on the landscape for eons and, until the 20th century, had its own way. It was at times benevolent and life-giving, at other times harsh and exacting as it jumped its banks in times of flood or dried up down river in times of drought.

Native Americans planted their crops in the moist silt deposits left along the banks of the river after annual floods. Early white settlers were quick to take advantage of the river by diverting it through canals into the broad, bowl-shaped Imperial Valley, which lies below the river to the west, to irrigate their crops. Man, by changing the natural patterns of the river, started a chain of events that brought about the taming of the Colorado River.

In 1905, the Colorado River broke through its banks and flowed, unchecked for two years, into the Imperial Valley. Levees were built and breached, rebuilt and breached again, until the river had created the 300 sq. mile Salton Sea.

Train car loads of materials were dumped from trestles by E.H. Harriman and his Union Pacific Railroad in an attempt to close the breach. For a time, materials moving by rail to stop the flooding of the Colorado River had precedence over all other rail freight. Harriman and the railroad efforts finally were successful, in 1907, and the river was contained.

The cycle of flood and drought continued after the river was returned to its natural course. The Colorado destroyed homes, farms and whole communities unlucky enough to be in its path. Controlling the river became the Bureau of Reclamation's main goal.

The bureau's engineers surveyed 70 sites as possible locations for a dam to control the Colorado. Finally, in 1924, Black Canyon was chosen to be the site of the most ambitious engineering project the world had ever seen–the harnessing of the Colorado River by the construction of Hoover Dam.

THE CONSTRUCTION OF HOOVER DAM...

The Boulder Canyon Project Act, passed by the U.S. Congress in 1928, provided $175 million for the construction of the dam, stipulating that the entire cost (including $25 million allocated as flood-control funds) be repaid to the government, with three percent interest, within 50 years. Revenues were to be generated by the sale of electric power generated by the dam. By 1976, final payment had been made to the government, a total gross of $378 million, representing a $202 million dollar profit for the government.

Hoover Dam, the official name for the dam since 1930 although the dam has always been equally referred to as Boulder Dam, presented engineering problems that were without precedence in the 1930s. The walls of Black Canyon rose at a sharply vertical angle for 800 feet above the Canyon floor. The nearest railroad was in Las Vegas, Nevada,

Above: The Colorado River at Needles.
PHOTO BY JERRY JACKA

more than 40 miles away, and the nearest source of sufficient electrical power was in San Bernardino, nearly 220 miles away. Everything, including labor, had to be imported.

In 1931, a consortium of companies, Six Companies, Inc., was awarded the contract for the construction of the dam. The successful bid was $48,890,995.50. A railroad was quickly constructed to bring materials to the site and a new town, Boulder City, was built to house construction workers and their families. At the height of construction, 5,218 people were employed by the Hoover Dam project.

Before construction of the dam could begin, the river had to be diverted. Four huge tunnels were bored into the canyon walls, two on each side, and two cofferdams were built, one upstream to divert the river to the tunnels, and one downstream to keep the river from flooding the construction site. Once the river was diverted, the construction area was

Left: Lake Powell, reaching depths of 560 feet, was formed by damming Glen Canyon.
PHOTO BY MICHAEL FATALI

pumped dry and water deposited silt was excavated down to bedrock. From this bedrock foundation a giant concrete, gravity-arch structure, the largest dam ever built at the time, was constructed.

Men were lowered down the canyon walls, placing dynamite charges to remove loose surface rock. Special "jumbo" rock drills were mounted on ten-ton trucks, each drill with 30 drill bits mounted to a platform, the largest drills ever assembled. Each time the operators guided the gigantic drills into the 56 foot diameter diversion tunnels, the holes were charged with dynamite and 2400 tons of rock were loosened. It took just under a year to drill all four tunnels. On November 14, 1932, the Colorado River was successfully diverted.

In the summer of 1933, with temperatures often above 120° Fahrenheit, the pouring of the concrete and the steel construction were under way. Two concrete plants were built and operated around the clock to fill the forms. Entire railroad cars of materials were lowered into the canyon by a gigantic tramway as men worked in shifts around the clock to keep up with construction.

The extreme temperatures, coupled with the exhausting task at hand, made it necessary to build a 60 bed hospital in Boulder City. At the dam itself, first-aid stations handled up to 1500 minor injuries each month.

Ninety-four construction workers and two government employees were killed working on Hoover Dam: 24 fell to their deaths; 10 were killed by explosions; five were electrocuted; three drowned; 26 were killed in machinery accidents; 26 were killed by falling debris; one died in a cableway accident; and one died in an elevator accident. In spite of all these tragedies, it has been said it is a testimonial

to the organizational skills of the project's managers that more people were not killed or seriously injured.

The most remarkable statistic is that the entire project; with more than 5,000 workers, 45 million pounds of steel, and five million barrels of concrete, took less than five years to complete. February 1, 1935, diversion tunnels were closed and Lake Mead began to fill.

Lake Mead has a capacity of more than 32 million acre feet of water. When full, it reaches

Above: London Bridge was transported, stone by stone, from London to Lake Havasu.
PHOTO BY BOB CLEMENZ

a depth of approximately 500 feet, is 110 miles long, and contains enough water to cover the entire state of New York to a depth of one foot.

The dam is a colossal 726.4 feet from the bedrock of Black Canyon to its top. It is 660 feet thick at its base and consists of more than 4,366,000 cubic yards of concrete, including the powerhouse and related structures.

Hoover Dam generates more than 2 million kilowatts of power. During its first 40 years of service, the dam generated approximately 150 billion kilowatts of power– enough power to supply a million homes for twenty years.

COMPARISON OF HOOVER DAM/LAKE MEAD AND GLEN CANYON DAM/LAKE POWELL

Hoover Dam/Lake Mead		Glen Canyon Dam/Lake Powell
Construction began:	April 1931	1956
Construction ended:	February 1935	1962
Height from bedrock:	726.4 feet	710 feet
Thickness at foundation:	660 feet	300 feet
Thickness at crest:	45 feet	25 feet
Crest length:	1,244 feet	1,560 feet
Total concrete:	4,360,000 cubic yards	4,901,000 cubic yards
Total Steel:	45,000,000 pounds	50,500,000 pounds
Surface area at capacity:	157,900 acres	161,000 acres
Storage capacity:	32,000,000 acre feet	25,000,000 acre feet
Length at capacity:	110 miles	190 miles
Maximum depth:	500 feet	560 feet

THE DESERT REGION

Arizona is home to more than sixty species of cacti including the stately Saguaro, *Carnegiea gigantea*. Saguaro are the largest cacti found in the United States, growing to heights of 50 feet, and may live for more than 200 years. The Saguaro flower is Arizona's state flower. It is against the law to uproot, or in any way damage, any cacti found in their natural surroundings.

The southwestern region of Arizona is the desert zone, consisting of broad, level plains that are bordered by mountains on two or more sides. Seldom over 2,000 feet in elevation, these desert valleys are not arid, sandy wastelands like most deserts. In most places, the valleys are river plains with deep, fertile top soil covered with drought resistant flora. The desert teems with wildlife, some species specially equipped to survive the harsh climate and others that migrate seasonally.

Water is the desert region's most precious resource. Where water flows, the desert grows. The earliest inhabitants in the region were the Hohokam, who first appeared around 300 BC. They occupied the region for about 1700 years and were the first farmers in the Southwest to exhibit a knowledge of irrigation, digging an extensive series of gravity-fed canals along the Gila and Salt rivers. After the Hohokam abandoned the desert region during the 15th century, the Pima, Spaniards and Mexicans irrigated farms along the Santa Cruz River, a tributary of the Gila.

The first major irrigation project by American settlers was undertaken in the Salt River Valley during 1867, by Jack Swilling, an ex-Confederate soldier who was an army deserter, reputed dope addict and reported murderer. Swilling noticed regular depressions running away from the Salt River and was convinced they were remains of ancient Indian irrigation canals.

Swilling raised $10,000 from prominent mine owners and investors and formed the Swilling Irrigation Canal Company. Water once again flowed through the same canals the Hohokam had built hundreds of years before. Over the decades following, it was determined many of the original Hohokam canals had been as much as 40 feet wide and 15 feet deep and were part of an overall system that included more than 200 miles of canals. Quite a construction feat in light of the Hohokam's primitive tools.

By summer of 1870, 300 people lived in the small town of Pumpkinville. As often happens, as a town grows the residents begin to put on airs. Locals decided the name was undignified and, at an 1870 town meeting, voted to change the name. The new name, the suggestion of Englishman Darrel Duppa, was chosen for the similarity between the legend of the Phoenix– a mystical bird that lived for 500 years, was consumed by fire, and rose anew from its own ashes– and the city, which was rising from the remains of an ancient civilization. Today, around 3 million people, more than half of the state's population, live in the greater Phoenix metropolitan area.

Desert region mountains are generally less than 4,000 feet in elevation and support sparse, drought resistant vegetation. Kitt Peak, in the Quinlan Mountains, is the site of the nation's largest federally supported observatory for optical astronomy. The Kofa Mountains, near Yuma, are a preserve for Bighorn Sheep and Arizona's only native palms. Tucson's Santa Catalina Mountains are world renowned for their dense Saguaro forest.

Preceding pages:, Gunsight and Padre Bay at Lake Powell is the site of "The Crossing of the Fathers," commemorating the Colorado River crossing by Franciscan missionaries,Fathers Escalante and Dominquez, in 1776.
PHOTO BY JERRY JACKA

Left: The Sonoran Desert in spring is carpeted with desert grasses, California poppies and blue lupine at South Mountain Park in Phoenix.
PHOTO BY DICK DIETRICH

Right: Saguaro, cholla and prickly pear cacti in foothills of the Lower Sonoran Zone at Saguaro National Monument in southern Arizona.
PHOTO BY DICK DIETRICH

THE APACHE CONFLICTS

Long before the arrival of the first European explorers, the Apache– Athabascan bands that migrated into the Southwest from the north– inhabited a territory ranging from the eastern slopes of the Rocky Mountains west to the base of the Sangre de Cristo Mountains (near Cimmaron and Las Vegas, New Mexico) and from the northern plains of the Colorado Plateau south to Mexico.

The Apache led simple existences during the centuries prior to the arrival of the Spanish Franciscan missionaries. They were a peaceful tribe who's subsistence depended on hunting, farming and foraging. Living in permanent villages, they conducted extensive buffalo hunts, grew maize (corn), and harvested great quantities of mescal. When necessary, they could literally "live off the land," hunting game animals and harvesting berries, roots, seeds and cacti.

The Apache were an extremely healthy and vigorous people prior to the introduction of European diseases. They were able to travel great distances, in the summer heat through the deserts or in chilling cold of winter in the mountains, with little or no discomfort.

With the Apache, past and present, women were held in high regard. They are protected, cherished and respected. Girls were given the same training as boys and practiced daily with bow and arrows, slings and spears. They were taught horseback riding and combat. During times of war, wives were permitted to go on the warpath with their husbands.

Contrary to popular belief, the Apache did not scalp their victims. In fact, the practice was introduced to Southwestern Native Americans by the Spanish. In the 1830s, the Spaniards instituted a scalp-bounty system, an ancient Spanish practice in which anyone bring in the scalp of an adult male would be paid $100, an adult female was worth $50, and the scalp of a child brought $25.

This practice backfired in many ways. It was impossible to differentiate between the scalp of an Apache and other Native Americans and soon even friendly tribes were on the warpath as unscrupulous bounty hunters collected scalps indiscriminately. Examining committees found it difficult to tell the difference between Indians and Mexican hair and soon entire Mexican villages were decimated so bounty hunters could collect their grisly rewards.

By 1837, the scalp hunting had escalated to unbelievable acts of depravity. Bounty hunter John Johnson illustrated the depths these despicable murderers would sink to in their quest for profit. Johnson entered the Apache village of San Jose, where he was well known, with a sack of gifts for the Apache. Inside one sack was a loaded canon with its barrel tightly plugged. When the Apache gathered around to see the "magic," Johnson lit the cannon fuse with a cigar and walked away. The canon exploded, killing almost all of the Apaches. Johnson and his men killed the rest and then calmly scalped the dead.

When an Apache was killed it obligated their next of kin to seek revenge. All large war parties were organized to avenge deaths. The Apache god, Usen, the supreme being described by both Geronimo and Cochise as the creator and ruler of all things, had not commanded the Apache to forgive their enemies. Nor was one life considered enough to avenge the death of an Apache–compensation would often require many lives. The great chief Cochise once stated; "You Americans began the fight, and now the Americans and Mexicans kill an Apache on sight. I have retaliated with all my might. I have killed ten white men for every Indian slain."

Continual harassment and encroachment by Spanish in Apache territory, conflicts with the Comanche, Mexican domination, American occupation of Apache ancestral grounds, and increasing pressures and controls placed on the Apache proved more than they could tolerate. The era of peaceful coexistence was brought to an abrupt end.

The great chiefs of the 1800s– Geronimo, Cochise, Mangas Coloradas, Nana, Loco and Victorio– led their bands in raids and warfare against the white intruders. With the Apache, raiding had always been a part of life. In raiding, the main objective was to gather food, horses and clothing. With warfare, fighting was the main objective, although the Apache would always bring home whatever plunder they could collect after a battle. Although there were countless skirmishes between the white man and Apache during the mid to late 1800s, in the final analysis the Apache were overcome by superior equipment, greater numbers and the use of Apache from other tribes as scouts against the bands remaining free.

Right: Wonderland of Rocks, Massai Point, in the Chiricahua National Monument.
PHOTO BY DAVID ELMS, JR.

COCHISE, CHIRICAHUA APACHE LEGEND

By the 1860s Cochise, Chiricahua Apache leader, was known as a shrewd strategist fearless warrior and by Americans, Mexicans and Indians alike. Son-in-law of famous Apache chief Mangas Coloradas, he was a strong and compassionate leader. Although Mexicans were terrified of him, he was a man of his word to all who knew him. At one time he held contracts to deliver wood to Butterfield Station in Apache Pass, where he was well respected.

In early 1861, rancher John Ward reported his stepson, Felix Ward, captured by Apaches. Even though there was no evidence linking abduction of the boy to Cochise's band, a company of U.S. Army Infantry, led by a young second lieutenant, George Bascom, contacted Cochise through an interpreter named Antonio. Cochise and several Apache went to Bascom's camp for a parley.

Cochise, and six Apache, entered a large tent with Bascom and several of his aides. In good faith, Cochise explained that his people had nothing to do with the missing boy, nor knew who the culprits were. As he spoke, Bascom's men surrounded the tent. Bascom informed Cochise that he and his men were under arrest. With lightning reflexes, Cochise pulled a knife and ripped through the rear of the tent, running at full speed toward freedom. The soldiers were caught completely unaware. By the time they regained their senses, and fired off more than 50 rounds, Cochise was out of range.

The Apache still in the tent, unable to escape, were taken prisoner. The next day Cochise tried to negotiate their release, as was Apache custom in such situations. When Lt. Bascom refused to leave the security of his camp, Cochise called to the Butterfield stationmaster, a stage driver and a hostler, who all knew and trusted him. Bascom refused to let the men go to Cochise, but they

"You Americans began the fight, and now the Americans and Mexicans kill an Apache on sight. I have retaliated with all my might. I have killed ten white men for every Indian slain."
— Cochise

started walking toward him anyway. Cochise moved to grab the men, not intending them harm but hoping to trade them for his six warriors. As the stationmaster was seized by the Indians, the other men panicked and ran. In the melee, Indians shot the driver, and soldiers, believing the innkeeper an attacking Indian, shot him.

That evening, Cochise and his band captured a small wagon train and took additional hostages. The next day Cochise, using the stationmaster as an interpreter, offered Bascom another trade, his hostages for Bascom's-plus Cochise would throw in 16 government mules.

Foolishly, Bascom refused unless the boy, who Cochise had never seen, was thrown in. As this charade continued over several days, Bascom continually received reinforcements. As Cochise gazed down on the scene from a hilltop vantage point, he knew the hostage trade talks were a stalling tactic and withdrew his band.

The hostages were left behind, all murdered and shockingly mutilated. When Bascom and his troops arrived on the grisly scene, he ordered the six Apache, and three additional Coyotero captives, hung. Cochise, wrongly accused of kidnapping young Felix Ward, was now on the warpath. The longer he contemplated the turn of events, the more furious he became.

Feeling there were no equitable dealings with the white man, Cochise spent the next 20 years on the warpath exacting revenge.

GERONIMO, APACHE GUERRILLA

Perhaps the most famous Apache warrior, Geronimo led the Bedonkohe Apache from their territory around the headwaters of the Gila River. Legendary for his bravery and tenacity, Geronimo was said, in numerous documented accounts, to have been clairvoyant. A story is told of Geronimo traveling home from a raid with a group of Mexican prisoners in tow, stopping, and suddenly saying to his band in a trance-like state, "Tomorrow afternoon, as we march back northward along the north side of the mountains, we will see a man standing on a hill to our left. He will howl to us and tell us that the troops have captured our base camp." The event occurred the next day just as Geronimo predicted.

Geronimo was never able to fully understand the contradictory nature of the white man, who would seize Apache lands with little regard for the Indians' rights. He wondered what gave these men the right to do this. Had their god given them these rights? The whites, Geronimo often mused, would plunder Apache lands, steal their horses, kill their people and destroy their villages. Why then did the white man think it so strange when the Apache responded in like measure?

In May of 1883, Geronimo surrendered for the first time to General George Crook, thought by most historians to be a fair, if somewhat harsh, man for his time. Upon taking office as the head of the Military Department in 1882, General Crook placed the blame for the Indian situation where it belonged. "Greed and avarice on the part of the whites, in other words the almighty dollar, is at the bottom of nine-tenths of all of our Indian problems." Geronimo, even though this first peace with the white man lasted for only three years, wanted to bring an end to the conflicts with the white man.

Geronimo in 1886.

In meeting General Crook the first time, Geronimo told Crook he felt the Apaches could fight indefinitely against Mexicans, killing them by using rocks instead of rifles if need be, a chore not unpleasant to Geronimo, who had lost two wives and four children to the Spanish by the 1850s. But, he explained to General Crook, once the Gray Fox (Crook) came, guided by his own people (Apache from other tribes), he knew that he must either make terms or die fighting.

General Crook made peace with Geronimo and accepted his surrender while granting favorable terms to the Apache. Unfortunately for all parties, Crook's terms were overridden in Washington and Geronimo, once again betrayed by the white man, was soon back on the warpath.

In 1881, Geronimo was again raiding with a band of 35 warriors, eight boys and 100 women and children. They killed 75 civilians, 12 Indians of other tribes, two officers, eight soldiers and more than 100 Mexicans. Geronimo was wounded many times and lost six men, two boys, a woman and a child. The campaign was made possible by Geronimo's mastery of guerrilla warfare.

By 1886, the U.S. had 5000 troops pursuing the last Apache bands. On September 4, 1886, Geronimo, the last Apache leader apprehended, surrendered his band to General Crook for the second and final time, ending the Apache wars.

General Crook offered Geronimo and his people two years in confinement, to be served outside the territory, after which they could return to the reservation and rejoin their families. But again, forces in Washington were not inclined to treat the Apache with honor. General Sheridan, with total disregard for Crook's promises, insisted on an unconditional surrender, and the permanent imprisonment of the Apache band.

General Crook replied he could not go back on his word to Geronimo and quickly resigned his command in protest. Geronimo was confined to prison in Florida until 1894, when his band was moved to the reservation at Fort Sill, Oklahoma, where he remained peacefully until his death on February 17, 1909.

ARIZONA AND THE CIVIL WAR

Although no conclusive Civil War battles were fought in Arizona, the war played a major role in the continuing development of the state. Until 1863, Arizona was part of the New Mexico Territory, which was comprised of lands that are now both New Mexico and Arizona. Because of its geographic position, the area was important to the Confederacy and its president, Jefferson Davis.

Davis wished to establish a link between Confederate territory in Texas, through the Southwest, to the Pacific Ocean. A port on the Pacific Ocean would provide an outlet to world markets free of the shackles of the Union blockade on the East Coast. In addition to establishing a coast to coast domain, which Davis felt would help the Confederate States to gain recognition as an independent nation with European countries, the South was in desperate need of the precious minerals found in California, Arizona, Nevada and Colorado.

The Civil War, in a roundabout way, was responsible for bringing law and order to the Arizona Territory. The Indians, thinking the white man had given up their battle to control the Indians when federal troops were withdrawn to fight the war in the East, became more aggressive. This withdrawal of federal presence caused remaining settlers, many of whom were from Southern states to begin with, to place their allegiance with the arriving Confederate troops sent under the leadership of Lieutenant Colonel John R. Baylor.

On August 1, 1861, Baylor proclaimed himself military governor of the "Confederate Territory of Arizona." Within a week of Baylor's arrival, a mass meeting was held in Tucson, where citizens voted to secede from the Union and elected Granville Oury as territorial representative to the Confederate Congress in Richmond, Virginia. On February 14, 1862, exactly fifty years before Arizona was granted statehood, it was officially made a Confederate territory.

Aroused by the Confederate interest in the Arizona Territory, Union troops under the command of Colonel Edward R.S. Canby were sent from New Mexico to engage Confederate troops under command of Major Henry H. Sibley who, interestingly enough, was the brother-in-law of Colonel Canby.

The struggle for control of Arizona proved to be more a contest of endurance– troops of both sides against the elements and hostile Indians–than an armed conflict against two opposing factions. The only battle to take place between North and South occurred at Picacho Peak, 45 miles northwest of Tucson.

Federal troops, commanded by Lieutenant James Barrett, learned that Confederate soldiers were in the vicinity of Picacho Peak. On April 15, 1862, the Union troops caught up with the unsuspecting Confederates and a short battle ensued. Two Union soldiers, and Lt. Barrett, were killed in the brief skirmish. Troops from both sides quickly withdrew in opposite directions, thus ending the westernmost conflict between the North and South of the Civil War.

The largest battle fought in Arizona during the Civil War occurred at Apache Pass, in July of 1862, as Federal troops were ambushed by Mangas Coloradas and Cochise. Two Union soldiers were killed, three were wounded and ten Apache were killed. The Apache saw little difference between Union and Confederate troops. Perhaps, if they had known the politics behind the scenes, they would have been inclined to have thrown their forces behind the Confederacy.

The Indians had used the confusion of the war to attempt to expel white settlers from their ancestral lands. The destruction and havoc they created was so savage that both Southern and Union leaders considered them a major obstacle in occupying the Southwest.

The Confederate governor of Arizona, Colonel Baylor, decided on a policy of extermination of the Indians. In a written order to Captain Helm, commander of the Tucson garrison, Baylor ordered Helm to use any means of persuasion, including the lure of whiskey, to bring the Indians in for peace talks. Once the Indians were judged drunk, all adult Indians were to be killed. The children were to be sold into slavery to recoup costs of the operation. The order, when it reached the hands of President Jefferson Davis, was rescinded and Baylor stripped of his command.

Below: Picacho Peak, 45 miles northwest of Tucson, was the site of the westernmost battle of the Civil War.
PHOTO BY DICK DIETRICH

THE LOST DUTCHMAN MINE

A frenzied whisper of "gold" spread swept through the camp like a wildfire on a summer day as Adolph Ruth wandered onto Tex Barkley's Quarter Circle U Ranch. Ruth had maps, old and very mysterious, said to have been penned by Jacob Waltz, the legendary, if not accurately named, Lost Dutchman. Supposedly, somewhere in the mountains adjacent to Barkley's ranch, was the famed Lost Dutchman's Mine and Ruth wanted Barkley's help to find a spot near a pointed peak in the heart of the Superstition Mountains, where the maps indicated the mine was located.

Barkley sighed and scratched his grizzled chin. This fortune hunter from back east was easily in his early sixties, and not in the best of shape. How would he ever survive the rugged trip into the Superstition Wilderness, let alone in the dead of summer? The heat was so scorching that even the nastiest rattlesnakes knew better than to venture out into the sun. But, the old man was so anxious, Barkley feared, that he might be crazy enough to strike out on his own, so Barkley agreed to take Ruth, but Ruth was too impatient to wait three days until Barkley could make the trip to Phoenix for supplies.

With two cowboy guides, Adolph Ruth set off in search of the Lost Dutchman's Mine without Barkley. That was the last time Tex Barkley saw Ruth alive. When he returned to his ranch and discovered Ruth gone, Barkley saddled up and went looking for him, fearing the worst– for Ruth had talked too much and to too many about his treasured maps, which he always kept close to his heart in a shirt breast pocket. Too many people have gold fever, thought Tex Barkley, and way too many would kill for a chance at the rumored riches of Jacob Waltz' Lost Dutchman's Mine.

Well into August the search continued for Adolph Ruth, as ranchers and sheriff's deputies spent long days in the blistering sun combing the area on horseback. They concentrated on the area around a peak called "Weaver's Needle," looking for a trace of the prospector's whereabouts, or his remains. Days stretched into weeks and still no trace of Adolph Ruth was found. After 45 days, the searchers gave up.

It wasn't until a chilly day in December that a Quarter Circle U ranch hand made a grisly find on a trek into the forbidding Superstitions. The partially decomposed skull turned out to be that of Adolph Ruth. Some claim there were bullet holes in the skull... others say he died of natural causes. One thing was sure, Adolph Ruth was dead, a casualty of the irresistible lure of the Lost Dutchman's Mine and its hidden gold.

It has been said that gold, like war, brings out the best and the worst in a man. Adolph Ruth died as another testimony to that fact.

THE GOLD RUSH OF THE 1860s

In spite of the ever-present danger of Indian attacks during the Civil War, prospectors searching northern Arizona's hills continued their quest for riches from the discovery of mineral deposits. Early in 1862, pay dirt was struck by Pauline Weaver, and others, just north of Ehrenburg. A town was established, near the trading post of Michael Goldwater, and miners swarmed the area.

La Paz, the new town, quickly became the most populated town in all of Arizona, with 1,500 residents living in tents and log houses. The boom quickly went bust as the difficulty of extracting the gold, and high prices charged by merchants for dry goods and liquor, made the miner's endeavors less than profitable.

The miner's attention moved to north-central Arizona, around the present sites of Prescott and Wickenburg. Jack Swilling and Henry Wickenburg, along with Captain Joseph R. Walker, located placers of gold and silver along Hassayampa, Big Bug, Lynx and Weaver creeks. Samples of pure gold were picked up on the surface along the creeks.

Jack Swilling, a member of Captain Walker's party, sent two samples of pure gold to General Carleton. The general, greatly excited and sure great gold fields were to be found within his domain, quickly sent the samples to the Secretary of the Treasury for presentation to President Lincoln.

Perhaps the richest gold deposits found in Arizona were at the Vulture Mine, discovered in 1863 by Henry Wickenburg, about 10 miles south of the town bearing his name today. With a background in geology, Wickenburg acted on rumors gold ore had been found in the Harquahala Mountains. Within a year of his mine's opening, he had more than 80 miners working his find. The town quickly grew to more than 200 residents, with the usual complement of dance hall girls, gunmen, gamblers and merchants.

Discovery of gold, based on Gen. Carleton's hastily sent reports, spurred Congress to annex Arizona as a Union territory. For a short time prospectors were literally finding gold laying on top of the ground in north-central areas of the state. Anxious to keep "vast gold fields" from Confederate hands, and needing to fill the Union's coffers, the government at last turned its attention, in 1863, to establishing Arizona as a territory separate from the New Mexico Territory.

Unfortunately, Arizona's gold deposits turned out to be shallow and the vast wealth the Union was expecting to find failed to materialize. In years following the Civil War, copper became the most important mineral in the state's economy. Gold, however, had already done its job in helping to establish Arizona along the way to statehood.

Above: Abandoned miner's cabin at Silver King.
PHOTO BY JERRY JACKA

LAW AND ORDER IN THE WEST

In the Southwest there was often a very thin line between the good guys and the bad. Control of frontier towns was often held by gamblers and gunmen, some who wore a badge. As mining and cattle ranching brought new riches into the Southwest, and cowboys' and miners' pockets were filled with wages, a sinister element arose to separate men from their money, and often their lives.

Saloons offered whiskey, gambling and women for recreation. Professional gamblers turned games of chance into fleecings. Tempers flared and working men died at the hands of the gamblers. Outlaws robbed banks, trains and stage-coaches regularly. Some men were as quick to kill others in a gun fight as they were to jump their claims or to steal their cattle. The man with the fastest six-gun was often a law unto himself.

Tombstone marshal Wyatt Earp was a lawman, gambler and gunfighter.

The story of Wyatt Earp and Doc Holliday illustrates the thin line between the good guys and the bad. Wyatt began his controversial career in law enforcement in 1870, when he was elected as constable in Lamar, Missouri. He resigned less than a year later and drifted south to Oklahoma, where he and two friends stole horses belonging to William Keys.

Earp and his companions were captured by a posse led by James Keys, William's brother, and placed under citizen's arrest. They were transported to Van Buren, Arkansas,

Above: The Tombstone Epitaph office in Tombstone, Arizona. The newspaper, founded in 1880, reported the famous gunfight at the OK Corral between the Earp and Clanton factions.
PHOTO BY DICK DIETRICH

where they faced charges as horse thieves. After posting a $500 bail, Wyatt fled the territory. By 1874, he was making a living as a gambler in Wichita, Kansas, where his brother, James, was tending bar. James' wife ran a bordello where Kate Elder, later Doc Holliday's mistress, was employed. Wyatt was elected as

a city policeman in Wichita's 1875 municipal election. When not involved with his official duties, he gambled and collected protection money from saloon keepers. Wyatt was fired when officials learned of his extortion racket, so he left town and followed the gambling circuit to Dodge City, where he once again became a law enforcement officer.

Wyatt Earp first met John Henry "Doc" Holliday, the dentist was a professional gambler, late in the winter

John Henry "Doc" Holliday, dentist and gunfighter.

of 1877. Lawman, gambler and gunfighter, Bat Masterson was also a close friend of Wyatt. The strong bond formed between Doc and Wyatt that was summed up by a quote from Masterson: "Doc's whole heart and soul were wrapped up in Wyatt Earp and he was always ready to stake his life in defense of any cause in which Wyatt was interested." The two would remain extremely close until Doc Holliday's death from tuberculosis in 1887.

While a lawman in Dodge City, Wyatt once again collected protection money. He owned interests in the Long Branch Saloon and the Alhambra Saloon. His only Dodge City gunfight resulting in death was in July of 1878. George Hoyt, a cowboy out on bail pending charges of cattle rustling, got into a drunken argument with a theater owner. He rode by the rear of the theater, firing shots at the building. As he rode away, Wyatt and Jim Masterson, Bat's brother, engaged him in a gunfight and took his life.

Bat Masterson was an Earp associate, gunfighter, lawman and later a reporter for a New York City newspaper.

Wyatt was rescued by Sheriff Bat Masterson as three rowdy Missourians attempted to assassinate him. The same men later tried to kill Masterson, who was tipped off by a friend. It is believed two of the men were the famous outlaws, Frank and Jesse James.

In 1879, Wyatt traveled to Las Vegas, New

"Mysterious Dave" Mather, outlaw and lawman, ran a fake gold brick scam in Mobeetie, Texas, with Wyatt Earp.

THE GUNFIGHT AT THE OK CORRAL

The Earp faction, Wyatt, Virgil, and Morgan Earp, along with their longtime friend, Doc Holliday, had long feuded with the Clanton-McLaury faction. Each accused the other of stagecoach robberies and murder. The evidence pointed to the Earps and Holliday. Tensions mounted until they reached a boiling point.

On October 25, 1881, Wyatt, Morgan and Doc Holliday cornered Ike Clanton and tried several times to incite him into a gunfight. Clanton was unarmed and left to get his gun. He returned and told Wyatt to be ready for a showdown in the morning. The next morning Virgil, the only Earp still a "lawman," pistol-whipped Ike and arrested him for carrying a gun within city limits. He was taken to court and fined $25. Tom McLaury came to the courthouse to aid Ike. As they left, Tom collided with Wyatt on the sidewalk, and Wyatt pistol-whipped McLaury for the accident.

At 2:30, the Earps and Holliday decided to gun down the Clantons and McLaurys. Sheriff John Behan attempted to calm the hostilities but was told by Virgil, "I will not arrest them, but will kill them on sight." The Earp-Holliday faction found Ike and Billy Clanton, Tom and Frank McLaury, and Billy Claiborne standing in a lot near the O.K. Corral, but not in the corral as the legend has it.

Virgil told the men to throw up their hands, causing them to reach for their guns. Claiborne broke and ran, handing his pistol to the unarmed Tom McLaury. Virgil shot Claiborne anyway. Frank McLaury was shot in the stomach and fatally wounded by Wyatt's first bullet. Holliday shot Tom McLaury in the chest and side with a sawed-off shotgun. Ike Clanton grabbed Wyatt's gun hand, pinned him against a wall, threw him to the ground and ran into a boarding house. Morgan shot Billy Clanton in the chest and Virgil shot him in the stomach. As Billy Clanton lay dying, he wounded Morgan in the neck and shoulder and Virgil in the leg.

In less than a minute the fight was over. Behan tried to arrest Wyatt, who refused to be arrested. The three dead men, Billy Clanton and Tom and Frank McLaury, were dressed in fine clothes and displayed in a store window with a sign stating, "murdered in the streets of Tombstone."

Tom and Frank McLaury, with Billy Clanton, on display in a hardware store window.

Mexico, via a stop in Mobeetie, Texas, with gambler friend "Mysterious Dave" Mather. The two men were run out of Texas by notoriously tough lawman, James McIntire, for swindling cowboys in a "gold brick" hoax. By the time Wyatt and his three brothers; James, Morgan and Virgil, arrived in Tombstone, Arizona, they were notorious throughout much of the Southwest.

Marshal Virgil Earp.

In 1880, Virgil Earp was appointed assistant marshal of Tombstone. Wyatt was dismissed from a similar position and was replaced by John H. Behan. Wyatt and Behan became bitter enemies, their feud further increasing when Behan's young mistress, Josephine Sarah Marcus, left him for Wyatt.

Wyatt Earp bought an interest in the Oriental Saloon and hired his brother Morgan, Doc Holliday, Luke Short, and Bat Masterson as dealers. The Earps were soon back to their old patterns of gambling and brawling. During this time it was charged that Doc Holliday, who had already killed several men, and the Earp brothers were responsible for several stage-coach robberies and a murder. The evidence did point strongly to Doc Holliday, including eye-witnesses' reports from and a sworn statement from Holliday's mistress, "Big Nose" Kate Elder, a woman of questionable morals. The person bringing these charges was rancher Ike Clanton who, along

Cattle rancher Ike Clanton was also a cattle rustler.

with his brother Billy and their friends Frank and Tom McLaury, was a known cattle rustler.

Ike Clanton testified against the Earp faction during a preliminary hearing. Wyatt, without a shred of evidence, countered that the robberies and murder were committed by Ike and Billy Clanton along with brothers Frank and Tom McLaury. As these inflammatory accusations flew, the stage was set for the most famous gunfight in history... The Gunfight at the OK Corral (see sidebar on page 78).

Morgan Earp was killed by four men, who shot him in the back, within a few months of the famous gunfight at the OK Corral.

Below: The Superstition Mountains.
PHOTO BY JERRY JACKA

ADDITIONAL POINTS OF INTEREST

Alamo Lake State Park... A 2500 acre fishing and water sports lake about 38 miles north of Wendon on the Bill Williams River.

Apache Trail... Famous trail running from Apache Junction to Globe.

Arizona Heritage Center... Headquarters for the Arizona Historical Society. Contains many excellent exhibits from Arizona's past.

Arizona-Sonoran Desert Museum... In the Tucson Mountains, features exhibits of desert flora and fauna.

Bisbee... 1880's copper mining town, tours are available.

Boyce-Thompson Arboretum... Desert plant specimens from around the world. Located between Florence Junction and Superior.

Casa Grande Ruins National Monument... Well preserved four-story Hohokam structure.

Cochise Stronghold... Hiding place of the famous Apache in the Dragoon Mountains.

Colossal Cave... Natural limestone wonder 28 miles southwest of Tucson.

Coronado National Memorial... Marks entry of Coronado into U.S., in 1540, in search of the Seven Cities of Cibola. South of Sierra Vista.

Desert Botanical Garden... Beautiful displays of desert plant life in natural surroundings. Located in Phoenix.

Fort Bowie National Historic Site... Major fort during the last century. Located in the town of Bowie.

Fort Huachuca... Now a major military base, the fort played an important role in territorial history. The museum is open to the public.

Fort Verde State Historic Park... Played an important part in 1870s Indian wars. Museum, buildings and homes open for inspection. Located in Camp Verde.

Heard Museum... Located in Phoenix. Fine examples of Native American arts and crafts with special emphasis on Southwestern tribes.

Heritage Square... Three-square-block park of fully-restored turn-of-the-century buildings and exhibits in downtown Phoenix

Hopi Villages... Walpi, Oraibi, Hotevilla and Shongopvi. Ceremonial dances, Hopi culture and history. Old Oraibi is thought the oldest village in North America. Located southeast of Tuba City.

Hubbell Trading Post... 1870's trading post still in operation today. Tours of John Lorenzo Hubbell's home. Near Ganado.

Jerome... Historic mining town. Museum and historical displays.

Kitt Peak National Observatory... Numerous large telescopes including famous McMath Solar Telescope. Located southwest of Tucson.

Lyman Lake State Park... 1500-acre lake, campgrounds and picnic sites near St. Johns.

Meteor Crater... Site of the impact of a giant meteor 25 miles west of Winslow.

Mission San Xavier del Bac... A Spanish mission established in 1700. Nine miles south of Tucson.

Montezuma Castle and Montezuma Well... Sinagua culture ruins near Camp Verde.

Museum of Northern Arizona... Displays natural history of northern Arizona, Native American arts and crafts. Located in Flagstaff.

Old Tucson... Old west movie town, displays and entertainment.

Organ Pipe National Monument... Scenic drive south of Ajo with spectacular views of Organ Pipe Cactus and pristine desert.

Painted Rock State Park... Indian petroglyphs and pictographs. Near Gila Bend.

Phoenix Zoo... Largest privately owned zoo in the United States.

Pioneer Arizona Museum... History of Arizona in the 1880's. Located 12 miles north of Phoenix.

Pipe Spring National Monument... Mormon Fort on the Honeymoon Trail. Near Kaibab.

Prescott Territorial Capital... Historic mining town and site of Arizona's first capital.

Pueblo Grande... Ancient Hohokam ruin and museum in Phoenix.

Sunset Crater National Monument... Volcanic crater near Flagstaff.

Yuma Territorial Prison... Housed criminals during the territorial days.

Tombstone... Famous old west silver mining town. Scene of the Gunfight at the OK Corral.

Tonto National Monument... Prehistoric cliff dwellings in excellent state of preservation. East of Roosevelt Dam on the Apache Trail.

Tubac State Historic Park... Ruins of Spanish military post and old adobe mission. Located south of Amado.

Tuzigoot National Monument... Ruin of the Sinagua culture, dated around AD 1300, two miles east of Clarkdale.

Walnut Canyon National Monument... Cliff dwellings in scenic canyon near Flagstaff.

Wupatki National Monument... 35,000 acres of prehistoric culture ruins. 25 miles north of Flagstaff.

Right: A winter snowstorm leaves Pinyon Pine and Utah One-seed Juniper of the Transition Zone near Sedona covered with snow.
PHOTO BY JERRY SIEVE

Below: The Kaibab Plateau at Murray Lake.
PHOTO BY CHARLES CHANLEY